# CHAPARRAL
# SHRUBS

*A Field Guide to the Common Chaparral Shrubs
of Southern California*

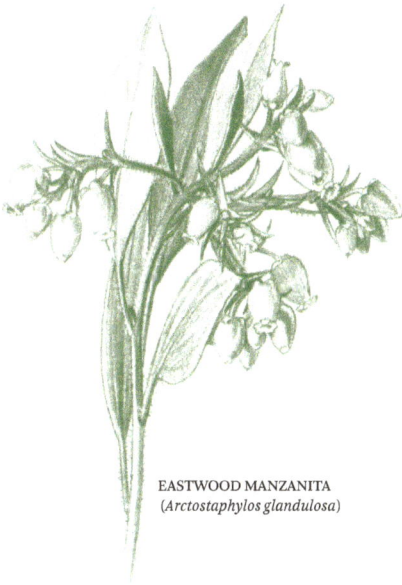

EASTWOOD MANZANITA
(*Arctostaphylos glandulosa*)

STEVE CHADDE

Approximate area of southern California covered by this guide. Chaparral vegetation is shown in dark green. Data from Cal Fire, Fire Resource and Assessment Program (FRAP).

CHAPARRAL SHRUBS
*A Field Guide to the Common Chaparral Shrubs of California*

Steve Chadde

An Orchard Innovations Field Guide
ISBN: 9781951682514

Printed in the United States of America

# CONTENTS

Typical California montane chaparral plant community, Santa Ynez Mountains, Santa Barbara County. Commonly known as "hard chaparral" due to dense stands of ceanothus (*Ceanothus* spp.), chamise (*Adenostoma* spp.), and scrub oak (*Quercus* spp.).

California is especially rich in plant species, subspecies, and varieties. Stebbins and Major (1965) reported more than 4000 species in California, one-third of these endemic. Currently, over 7000 species are reported for the state, with somewhat more than 2000 species considered as endemic (BONAP, 2020). Such richness is largely attributable to the extreme diversity of habitats and conditions created by the climate and geology of California. It is not uncommon to find habitats that contain isolated or disjunct populations that are geographically separated from the main population center for that species.

Plant species and habitat diversity figures importantly in the implementation of sound land management practices. The best decisions of the land manager are those which account for the vegetation of an area; that is, species identification, habitat distribution, responses to fire, and value as food for wildlife or livestock grazing. But not all land managers are botanists. This guide is therefore directed to the land manager who has some biology training but not a strong background in technical plant identification. Moreover, it is designed as a field identification manual of 132 of the most important and/or most common shrubs in the southern California chaparral area. However, this guide is not intended to replace standard taxonomy manuals such as McMinn (1939) or Munz (1974), nor is it a source document for all southern California shrubs.

Vegetative and woody parts of plants have been used in building the keys to the species. Those familiar with plant keys know that many species are distinguished by their flowering and fruiting characteristics. Often, the only consistent difference between two species is floral. Users of this guide are encouraged to treat any identification as tentative until a specimen is identified by a qualified botanist who will often use standard taxonomic references such as McMinn (1939), Munz and Keck (1959), or Munz (1974). When necessary, the collected specimen should be verified against herbarium specimens.

The plant key is most reliably applied to the following foothills and ranges of southern California: the southern part of the south coastal ranges and the Santa Ynez, Santa Monica, and San Gabriel Mountains of Santa Barbara, Ventura, Los Angeles, and Orange Counties; the San Bernardino and San Jacinto Mountains of San Bernardino Riverside Counties; and the Santa Rosa, Santa Ana, Palomar, Cuyamaca, and Laguna Mountains of Riverside, San Diego, and Orange Counties.

# INTRODUCTION

## Plants Included in the Guide

This guide emphasizes shrub species on the coastal drainage side of the mountains of California (cismontane) as opposed to the desert side (transmontane). The transition between coastal drainage species and desert species is gradual.

Shrubs or subshrubs fitting the following conditions are included:

• Plants with main stems that are woody at least at the base, usually living several years or more;

• Plants with several main branches from or near the ground. If these conditions do not apply, then the plant is probably not included in this guide, with the following exceptions:

   • *Yucca* species which commonly have short woody stems but are prominent members of the chaparral community;

   • Several species of vines that climb over and through other shrubs but have mostly woody stems;

   • A few species normally considered trees but often existing in multiple-stem shrub form.

## How to Use the Vegetative Keys

The vegetative keys identify shrubs based solely on vegetative characters. Thus, it is important to study the leaves and stems carefully. Choose a leaf whose size and shape looks like at least two-thirds of the leaves on the shrub. In other words, look at several leaves. Avoid young or immature leaves which often differ from mature leaves. Major leaf features are illustrated on page 320. Determine whether the leaves on your specimen are scale-like or not scale-like. Are the leaves alternate or opposite" Are the leaf veins in a pinnate or palmate pattern? Are the leaves simple or compound? If they are compound are they palmate or pinnate?

Begin with page 7 of the vegetative key and find the correct group, subgroup, and leaf type; then in the section directed to compare statement a with statement b at the same level of indentation. The number sequence is only important relative to statements a and b, the comparison statements must have the same number. Also the further along in the key, the higher the number. If your specimen best fits statement b, go directly down one line under b and one indentation to the right to the next statement a, and compare this statement a and statement b with your specimen. Continue making these dichotomous comparisons until the comparison ends with the name of a shrub species or genus. Go to the page indicated and you will find either a genus or species description. If you are at the genus level, you will either go through another dichotomous key to get to the species or you will need to select the description which most closely fits your specimen. If you are directed to a species compare your specimen with the description and illustration.

## Vegetative Key to Common Southern California Shrubs

GROUP I. Plants vine-like with woody stems that climb through and over other shrubs and trees.................................................go to 1a

GROUP II. Plants not vine-like; leaves stiff, sharp-pointed, spine-tipped, often more than 30 cm long. ........................ YUCCA (*Yucca* spp.), page 312

GROUP III. Plants not vine-like, leaves not stiff and sharp-pointed; stems mostly woody.

  SUBGROUP I. Leaves scale-like, less than 6 mm long. .............go to 7a

  SUBGROUP II. Leaves usually more than 3 mm long, not scale-like.

   LEAF TYPE I. Leaves opposite; that is, paired with one on each side of the stem. ...................................................go to 9a

   LEAF TYPE II. Leaves simple and alternate, lanceolate or oblanceolate or segments nearly linear; leaves mostly less than 11 mm wide, up to 22 mm wide if leaves approach 15 cm long (secondary and terminal stems of *Spartium junceum* are green, vaguely rush-like; leaves tend to be drought deciduous by May or June).......................go to 27a

   LEAF TYPE III. Leaves simple, alternate, mostly more than 10 mm wide; leaf may have several veins arising from near the base, and/or with leaves that are palmately lobed...........................go to 49a

   LEAF TYPE IV. Leaves simple, alternate, mostly more than 10 mm wide, pinnately veined with one main vein from the base or with several veins arising from the base with sparse branching; mature leaves tough and/or stiff and thick and/or leathery..................... go to 62a

   LEAF TYPE V. Leaves simple, alternate, mostly more than 10 mm wide, pinnately veined or with several veins with sparse branching arising from the base of long, narrow lance or linear shaped leaves; mature leaves more or less of thin and flexible feel.................go to 82a

   LEAF TYPE VI. Leaves alternate, mostly more than 10 mm wide, and compound; that is, leaves are divided into leaflets in a palmate or pinnate arrangement. ..........................................go to 99a

   LEAF TYPE VII. Leaves whorled, three at a node on the stems; subshrub on dry slopes in pine and oak woodlands and in manzanita chaparral. ...........WHORL-LEAF PENSTEMON (*Keckiella ternata*), page 172

# VEGETATIVE KEY

GROUP I. Plants vine-like with woody stems that climb through and over other shrubs and trees.

1a. Stems prickly; widespread shrubs in woodlands and chaparral. . . . . . . . . . .
. . . . . . . . . . . . . . . . . . . . . . . . . . . . . . . . . . **BLACKBERRY** (*Rubus* spp.), page 260
1b. Stems not prickly.
   2a. Leaves alternate.
      3a. Leaves divided into three leaflets; widespread shrub on shaded slopes. . . . . . . . . **POISON-OAK** (*Toxicodendron diversilobum*), page 298
      3b. Leaves not divided, with five main veins from the base; occasional shrub along shaded streams. . **WILD GRAPE** (*Vitis girdiana*), page 308
   2b. Leaves opposite, arranged in definite pairs along the stems.
      4a. Leaves compound, usually divided into more than three leaflets; occasional shrub on shaded, mesic slopes and along streams, in many plant communities. . . **WESTERN CLEMATIS** (*Clematis* spp.), page 108
      4b. Leaves simple, not divided into leaflets.
         5a. Leaves shiny and dark green above, thin and/ or flexible, none are united.
            6a. Leaves cordate to ovate with serrate margins; widespread shrub in dry chaparral to oak woodlands. . . . . . . . . . . . . . . . . .
. . . . **STRAGGLY PENSTEMON** (*Keckiella cordifolia*), page 170
            6b. Leaves round to ovate not cordate, entire margins; common shrub on shaded woodland and chaparral slopes. . . . . .
. . . . . . . . . . . . **SNOWBERRY** (*Symphoricarpos* spp.), page 294
         5b. Leaves usually dark green, not especially shiny, but thick, leathery, and not flexible; leaves near the end of stems and below the inflorescence may be united around the stem; dry chaparral to conifer forests. . . . . . . . **HONEYSUCKLE** (*Lonicera* spp.), page 181

GROUP III. Plants not vine-like, leaves not stiff and sharp-pointed; stems mostly woody.

SUBGROUP I. Leaves scale-like and less than 6 mm long.
7a. Leaves completely covering the branchlets and closely adhering; branches crooked; dry coastal washes and desert slopes. . . . . . . . . . . . . . . . . . . . . . **JUNIPER**
. . . . . . . . . . . . . . . . . . . . . . . . . . . . . . . . . . . . . . . . . . (*Juniperus* spp.), page 163
7b. Leaves scattered along the branchlets.
   8a. Leaves located singly on the stems; stems straight and broom-like; coastal washes and desert slopes. . . . . . . . . . . . . . . . . . . . . . . **SCALEBROOM**
. . . . . . . . . . . . . . . . . . . . . . . . . . . . . . (*Lepidospartum squamatum*), page 178
   8b. Leaves in twos and threes appearing as brown or blackish rings at the joints of the branches; subshrub, desert slopes. . . . . . . . . . . **MORMON-TEA**
. . . . . . . . . . . . . . . . . . . . . . . . . . . . . . . . . . . . . . . . . . (*Ephedra* spp.), page 124

SUBGROUP II. Leaves usually more than 3 mm long and not scale-like.

LEAF TYPE I. Leaves opposite; that is, paired with one on each side of the stem.

**9a.** Leaves compound, pinnately divided into 3 to 9 glaucous to pubescent leaflets.

> **10a.** Young stems feel round when rolled between the fingers; widespread shrub in canyons and valleys. .... **ELDERBERRY** (*Sambucus* spp.), page 284
>
> **10b.** Young stems feel square; fuzzy with fine hairs; shrub, chaparral and riparian communities.............. **FLOWERING ASH (FOOTHILL ASH)** ........................................(*Fraxinus dipetala*), page 146

**9b.** Leaves simple, not compound as above.

> **11a.** Leaves aromatic, with a strong smell when crushed.
>
> > **12a.** Leaves 1 to 3 mm wide, flat; stems more or less round throughout the plant; shrub, coastal sage scrub to chamise chaparral on coastal bluffs and desert slopes.. **BUSHRUE** (*Cneoridium dumosum*), page 110
> >
> > **12b.** Leaves more than 3 mm wide and/ or rolled under at edges, stems usually squarish, subshrubs.
> >
> > > **13a.** Leaves nearly linear to narrowly lanceolate, up to 6 mm wide, becoming strongly rolled under at edges; widespread on dry coastal mountain slopes. ............... **WOOLLY BLUE CURLS** ...........................(*Trichostema lanatum*), page 300
> > >
> > > **13b.** Leaves more than 6 mm wide and elliptic to lanceolate.
> > >
> > > > **14a.** Leaf veins noticeably prominent and leaves usually more than 2 cm wide; open chaparral and woodlands on dry slopes. .......... **PITCHER SAGE** (*Lepechinia calycina*), page 176
> > > >
> > > > **14b.** Leaf veins not especially prominent and leaves mostly narrower; widespread in chamise chaparral to coastal and desert sage scrub............. **SAGES** (*Salvia* spp.), page 274

> **11b.** Leaves not aromatic, lacking a strong smell when crushed.
>
> > **15a.** Plants with warty projections on the stems at the base of the leaves; leaves often notched at the tips or cupped upwards; widespread shrubs. .................... **CALIFORNIA-LILACS** (*Ceanothus* spp.), page 74
> >
> > **15b.** Plants without warty projections; leaves not as above.
> >
> > > **16a.** Leaves mostly flat, feel thin and/or flexible.
> > >
> > > > **17a.** Plant thorny with many sharp-tipped twigs in opposite branching from the main stems; leaves small and falling early; shrub, dry flats and canyons, San Diego County and south. .......... **ADOLPHIA** (*Adolphia californica*), page 32
> > > >
> > > > **17b.** Plant not thorny, leaves not falling early.
> > > >
> > > > > **18a.** Leaves up to 12 cm long and 6 cm wide, large shrubs or small trees up to 6 m tall.
> > > > >
> > > > > > **19a.** Leaves lanceolate to elliptic or oblanceolate, leaf tips pointed with obvious lateral veins that curve toward the tip.

**20a.** Young twigs may be reddish with a few stiff short hairs; if not reddish, then twigs covered with short hairs; leaves glabrous or nearly so, not glandular; robust montane shrub 2 to 5 m tall, moist woodlands. . . . . . . . . . . **DOGWOOD**
. . . . . . . . . . . . . . . . . . . (*Cornus* spp.), page 114

**20b.** Young stems yellowish green becoming light brown, leaves glandular and often somewhat sticky; subshrub 0.3 to 1.2 m tall, dry slopes, coastal sage scrub to chaparral. . . . . . .
**MONKEYFLOWER** (*Diplacus longiflorus*), p. 118

**19b.** Leaves elliptic to ovate, leaf tip more or less rounded without especially obvious veins, veins do not curve toward leaf tip, twigs whitish to grayish; occasional in moist montane canyon bottoms. . . . .
**BURNING BUSH** (*Euonymus occidentalis*), page 144

**18b.** Leaves all less than 5 cm long and up to 4 cm wide.

**21a.** Leaves grayish green to light green, round to ovate with blunted end, pubescent above and below, rarely only on the margins; shrub, woodland and shaded chaparral slopes. . . . . . . . . . . **SNOWBERRY**
. . . . . . . . . . . . . . . . . (*Symphoricarpos* spp.), page 294

**21b.** Leaves green, lance-ovate to roundish, usually with more or less pointed end, glabrous to minutely pubescent.

**22a.** Leaves entire, linear to ovate-elliptic, up to 2 cm long, 0.7 cm wide; spreading and much-branched shrub, common on dry rocky sage scrub and chaparral slopes. **BUSH PENSTEMON**
. . . . . . . . . . (*Keckiella antirrhinoides*), page 168

**22b.** Leaves with coarse or fine serrated margins, ovate to roundish leaves, usually with heart-shaped base, 1.5 to 5 cm long, 1 to 3 cm wide; sprawling, vine-like shrub, dry oak woodland and chaparral slopes. . . . . . . . . . . . . . . . .
. . . . . . . . . . . . . . . . . **STRAGGLY PENSTEMON**
. . . . . . . . . . . . . . (*Keckiella cordifolia*), page 170

**16b.** Leaves rolled under along margins; feel thick, tough and leathery.

**23a.** Some leaves long and narrow, up to five times longer than broad; subshrub 0.3 to 1.2 m tall, dry coastal sage scrub to chaparral slopes. . . . . . . . . . . . . . . . . . **MONKEYFLOWER**
. . . . . . . . . . . . . . . . . . . . . . . (*Diplacus longiflorus*), page 118

**23b**. Leaves wider, usually less than five times longer than broad.

  **24a**. Erect, more or less rigid shrubs.

    **25a**. Young stems usually more or less white, woolly, not especially stiff; scattered shrub on dry chaparral slopes. . . . . **SILKTASSEL** (*Garrya veatchii*), page 150

    **25b**. Young stems considerably pubescent but not woolly; rigid shrub on dry barren slopes near and in desert. . . . . . . . . . . . . . . . . . . . . . **JOJOBA (GOATNUT)** . . . . . . . . . . . . . . . . . . (*Simmondsia chinensis*), p. 288

  **24b**. Plant not especially woody, often not erect throughout, either decumbent and straggly, vine-like or with more or less brittle stems, mainly woody below.

    **26a**. Branches straggly or twining, often climbing through other shrubs; dry chaparral to conifer forests. . . **HONEYSUCKLE** (*Lonicera* spp.), page 181

    **26b**. Branches not as above, erect and rounded subshrub with harsh more or less resinous surfaces; dry chaparral and coastal sage scrub in southwestern San Diego County. . . . . . . **SAN DIEGO SUNFLOWER** . . . . . . . . . . . . . . . . . . . . . . (*Bahiopsis laciniata*), p. 68

**LEAF TYPE II**. Leaves are simple and alternate, lanceolate or oblanceolate or segments nearly linear. Leaves mostly less than 11 mm wide, up to 22 mm wide if leaves approach 15 cm long (secondary and terminal stems of *Spartium junceum* are green, vaguely rush-like. Leaves tend to be drought-deciduous by May or June).

**27a**. Leaves usually present and definitely linear, or narrowly lance-shaped or narrow spatulate.

  **28a**. Leaves deeply divided into linear lobes but not compound.

    **29a**. Leaves and stems green and resinous; bark reddish gray, shredded, peeling; dry chaparral, often in well-defined plant communities. . . . . **RED SHANK (RIBBON BUSH)** (*Adenostoma sparsifolium*), page 30

    **29b**. Leaves gray green; bark not as above.

      **30a**. Leaves aromatic, with a strong sage-like smell; upper leaves maybe linear and fascicled; subshrub, common on dry exposed coastal sage scrub slopes. . . . . . . . . . . . . . . . **COAST SAGEBRUSH** . . . . . . . . . . . . . . . . . . . . . . . . . . . . . . . (*Artemisia californica*), page 52

      **30b**. Leaves lacking a strong smell, at least some leaves divided, not fascicled; subshrub in dry washes and slopes, coastal sage scrub to scrub oak chaparral. . . . . . . . . . . . . . **BUSH GROUNDSEL** . . . . . . . . . . . . . . . . . . . . . . . . . . . . . (*Senecio flaccidus*), page 286

**28b.** Leaves not divided into linear lobes.

    **31a.** Branches rather straight and broom-like.

        **32a.** Stems and leaves whitish green; subshrub, dry open montane conifer slopes. . . . . . . . . . . . . . . . . . . . . . . . . . . . . . . . . . . . . . . . . . . .
. . . . . . . **RUBBER RABBITBRUSH** (*Ericameria nauseosa*), page 130

        **32b.** Stems and leaves green, resinous; maybe nearly leafless except near end of stems; shrub, sandy washes, San Diego County and south. . . **BROOM BACCHARIS** (*Baccharis sarothroides*), p. 66

    **31b.** Branches not as above.

        **33a.** Branches thorny, more or less sharp-tipped; leaves may be in fascicles, almost linear to spatulate (oblanceolate).

            **34a.** Leaves single or in groups of three; numerous spine-tipped short branchlets; intricately-branched shrub; coastal shrub, mostly below 110 m elevation. . . . . . . . . . . . . . . . . . . . .
. . . . . . . . . . . . . . **BOXTHORN** (*Lycium californicum*), page 188

            **34b.** Leaves generally in fascicles (bundles) with short and long leaves together; branches somewhat spine tipped; shrub, desert slopes. **DESERT ALMOND** (*Prunus fasciculata*), p. 206

        **33b.** Branches not thorny or sharp-tipped; short, needle-like leaves in fascicles, 4 to 10 mm long; most common chaparral shrub. . . .
. **CHAMISE (GREASEWOOD)** (*Adenostoma fasciculatum*), page 28

**27b.** Leaves wider than above, up to 10 mm wide (up to 22 mm if leaves approach 15 cm long). Leaves sometimes nearly missing but then leaving small green twigs.

    **35a.** Leaves usually present and strongly aromatic.

        **36a.** Leaves whitish, not resin dotted.

            **37a.** Leaves with three or more short teeth at tips, widest point may exceed 10 mm; shrub, desert interface scrub communities, dry conifer woodlands. . . . . . . . . . . . . . . . . . **BASIN (BIG) SAGEBRUSH**
. . . . . . . . . . . . . . . . . . . . . . . . . . . . . . (*Artemisia tridentata*), page 54

            **37b.** Leaves usually deeply divided into linear (1 mm wide) segment; common subshrub, dry coastal sage scrub, chaparral washes and slopes. . . . . . . . . . . . . . . . . . . . . . . **COAST SAGEBRUSH**
. . . . . . . . . . . . . . . . . . . . . . . . . . . . . (*Artemisia californica*), page 52

        **36b.** Leaves green, more or less resin-dotted, sticky, lemon or pine smell; some or most leaves less than 2 mm wide; shrub, dry coastal sage scrub; chaparral washes and slopes. . . . . . . . . . . . . . . **GOLDENBUSH**
. . . . . . . . . . . . . . . . . . . . . . . . . . . . . (*Ericameria pinifolia*), page 134

    **35b.** Leaves, if present, not strongly aromatic.

        **38a.** Leaves usually present, most lance shaped; mature leaves usually more than 4 cm long.

**39a.** Leaves dark green on both surfaces, somewhat sticky, often appearing three-veined with the lowest laterals continuing to near leaf tip; common willow-like evergreen shrub, streamsides and other wet places. . . . . . . . **MULE FAT** (*Baccharis glutinosa*), page 62

**39b.** Leaves somewhat tomentose to silky, white hairs, midvein with several laterals throughout its length; common deciduous shrub, wet places. . . . **SANDBAR WILLOW** (*Salix exigua*), page 270

**38b.** Leaves, if present, mostly less than 6 cm long; not lance-shaped.

**40a.** Leaves usually present; at least some in fascicles.

**41a.** Leaves more or less revolute or at least rolled under at the edge.

**42a.** Leaves tend to be wedge-shaped or rounded to heart-shaped with point at end.

**43a.** Leaves generally have three broad, blunt teeth at end; glabrous or nearly so, more or less glandular; shrub, desert and chaparral-desert interface. . . . . . . . . . . . **BITTERBRUSH** (*Purshia tridentata*), page 212

**43b.** Leaves round or heart-shaped; subshrub, coastal bluffs. . . . . . . . . . . . **SEACLIFF BUCKWHEAT** . . . . . . . . . . . . . . . (*Eriogonum parvifolium*), page 142

**42b.** Leaves longer, not wedge-shaped, tapering to a point, pubescent, not glandular; low, spreading shrub, dry slopes. . . . . . . . . . . . . . . **CALIFORNIA BUCKWHEAT** . . . . . . . . . . . . . . . . . . (*Eriogonum fasciculatum*), page 140

**41b.** Leaves normally flat or at least not rolled under at the edges.

**44a.** Leaves tend to be more or less round or oval on a petiole at least 2 mm long; evergreen shrub, dry coastal sage scrub slopes. . **REDBERRY** (*Rhamnus crocea*), p. 222

**44b.** Leaves more or less long and narrow, normally sessile.

**45a.** Leaves and at least some twigs are pubescent to densely tomentose; leaves not resinous and sticky.

**46a.** Leaves almost all less than 3 mm wide, rigid and spine-tipped with age; branchlets and leaves light gray to white with tomentum, darkening with scale patches during aging; shrub, dry slopes. . . . . . . . . . . . **HAIRY HORSEBRUSH** . . . . . . . . . . . . . . (*Tetradymia comosa*), page 296

**46b.** Leaves 2 to 8 mm wide, becoming neither spine-tipped or very rigid with age: branchlets covered with white or rusty star shaped hairs, mixed with straight hairs, becoming grayish with age but without scale spots; small shrub, dry montane flats and desert..... **WINTERFAT** ............ (*Krascheninnikovia lanata*), p. 174

> **45b.** Leaves and twigs glabrous or nearly so, resinous and sticky; erect shrubs, dry exposed south slopes and washes...................... **GOLDENBUSH** .................. (*Ericameria parishii*), page 132

**40b.** Leaves, if present, are not in fascicles.

> **47a.** Leaves, if present, are green and glabrous.
>
> > **48a.** Leaves present, often appear to be three-veined; leaves and young stems more or less glandular; shrub may have broom-like appearance; shrubs and subshrubs, many environments. **BACCHARIS** (*Baccharis* spp.), p. 60
> >
> > **48b.** Leaves, if present, nearly flat, green and neither glandular or pubescent; both secondary and terminal branches are green becoming gray at base; plant, more or less delicate with vague rush-like appearance, naturalized exotic shrub, roadsides. ........ **SPANISH BROOM** ....................... (*Spartium junceum*), page 290
>
> **47b.** Leaves mostly grayish and scurfy, not glandular, definite single midvein; shrub, dry hills and washes, desert and chaparral-desert interface. **SALTBUSH** (*Atriplex canescens*), page 56

**LEAF TYPE III.** Leaves simple, alternate, mostly more than 10 mm wide, several veins arising near the base and/or with leaves palmately lobed.

**49a.** Leaves with three or more veins coming from the base, not palmately lobed.

> **50a.** Several veins arising from the base of the leaf.
>
> > **51a.** Leaves rounded, mostly with six, seven, or more main veins from base; shrub or small tree; Palomar, Laguna, and Cugamaca Mountains. ............................ **REDBUD** (*Cercis occidentalis*), page 98
> >
> > **51b.** Leaves usually longer than broad, with three veins arising from the base; common shrub, many communities. .... **CALIFORNIA-LILACS** ....................................... (*Ceanothus* spp.), page 74
>
> **50b.** Leaves with three to five veins arising from near the base of single central vein.
>
> > **52a.** Leaves triangular to lance-shaped; leaves and stems harsh and roughly hairy; subshrub, dry chaparral and coastal sage scrub, southwestern San Diego County. ............... **SAN DIEGO SUNFLOWER** ..................................... (*Bahiopsis laciniata*), page 68
> >
> > **52b.** Leaves and stems not as above.
> >
> > > **53a.** Leaves notched or somewhat heart-shaped at base.

**54a.** Leaves 1.2 to 4 cm long; plant aromatic with many thin stems from a woody base; subshrub, dry coastal sage scrub to chamise chaparral washes and slopes. .... **BRICKELLBUSH** ........................... (*Brickellia californica*), page 72

**54b.** Leaves 3 to 15 cm long; plant not aromatic, sparingly branched; subshrub, shaded canyon sides, coastal sage scrub to scrub oak chaparral. ............ **CANYON-SUNFLOWER** ....................... (*Venegasia carpesioides*), page 306

**53b.** Leaves not as above, rounded or tapering at base.

**55a.** Leaves yellowish green and pubescent; bark light brown; subshrub, coastal bluffs, coastal sage scrub to dry chaparral. ...... **CALIFORNIA ENCELIA** (*Encelia californica*), page 120

**55b.** Leaves covered with dense hairyness; leaf feels of felt; subshrub, interior species, dry chaparral to deserts......... .... **BRITTLEBUSH (INCIENSO)** (*Encelia farinosa*), page 122

**49b.** Leaves with single vein at the base, may branch later, at least obscurely palmately lobed to deltoid to nearly round, but with three or more rounded or pointed lobes in outline.

**56a.** Stems with spines where the leaves are attached; widely distributed shrub........................... **GOOSEBERRIES** (*Ribes* spp.), page 234

**56b.** Stems lacking spines.

**57a.** Leaves with three to five pinnate lobes, pinnate venation, olive colored; stems exude clear bitter juice; subshrub, dry coastal sage scrub and chaparral washes and canyons. ............... **MATILIJA POPPY** ...................................... (*Romneya* spp.), page 252

**57b.** Leaves may be variously lobed but not generally in pinnate form, green; stems lack bitter juice.

**58a.** Leaves dark green above, rusty, fuzzy below, on branchlets; usually with well-developed thick trunk at base large shrub or small tree, chaparral to conifer slopes.......... **FLANNEL BUSH** .................... (*Fremontodendron californicum*), page 148

**58b.** Leaves and stems not as above; basal branches usually less than 2 cm thick; not trunk-like, but may be up to 5 cm in *Malacothamnus*.

**59a.** Leaves grayish green, densely fuzzy on both surfaces; shrub, dry coastal sage scrub canyon sides.. **BUSH MALLOW** .................. (*Malacothamnus fasciculatus*), page 190

**59b.** Leaves not as above; lacking fuzz; if fuzzy, then green above and paler below.

**60a.** Leaves less than 10 cm wide, lobes rounded in outline; widely distributed shrub. ............ **CURRANTS** ................................ (*Ribes* spp.), page 234

**60b.** Leaves more than 10 cm wide with three or more lobes.

> **61a.** Leaves 10 to 16 cm wide, 3 to 5 blunt lobes; stems not armed; bark grayish, peeling; young branchlets may be pubescent; shrub, open woods, shaded canyons. . . . . . . . . . . . . . . **THIMBLEBERRY** . . . . . . . . . . . . . . . . . . . . (*Rubus parviflorus*), page 264
>
> **61b.** Leaves large, 10 cm up to 40 cm, more than five lobes; stems glabrous, often red and herbaceous; exotic subshrub, washes and waste places. . . . . . . . . . . . . . **CASTOR-BEAN** (*Ricinus communis*), page 250

**LEAF TYPE IV.** Leaves simple, alternate, mostly more than 10 mm wide, pinnately veined with one main vein from the base or with several veins arising from the base with sparse branching; mature leaves tough and/or stiff and thick and/or leathery.

**62a.** Leaves stiff, mostly spiny or at least with sharply serrated margins.

> **63a.** Leaves clasping the stems at base, lacking petiole; low subshrub, open hills, coastal sage scrub to chamise chaparral. . . . . . . . . . . . . . . . . . . . . . . . . . . . . . . **SAWTOOTH GOLDENBUSH** (*Hazardia squarrosa*), page 154
>
> **63b.** Leaves petioled, at least not clasping stems.

> > **64a.** Mature leaves of various lengths up to 13 cm long.

> > > **65a.** Leaves green, lighter below and usually hairless but sometimes pubescent; leaves usually flat, sometimes convex, bark becoming gray but not shreddy; large shrub or tree, shaded chaparral to oak woodland slopes. . . . . . **TOYON (CHRISTMASBERRY)** . . . . . . . . . . . . . . . . . . . . . . . . . . . (*Heteromeles arbutifolia*), page 156
> > >
> > > **65b.** Leaves green, white fuzz below and hairless above; leaves usually strongly revolute, sometimes flat; bark becoming gray and shreddy; shrub, dry chaparral slopes below 550 m near coast. . . . . . . . . . **SUMMER-HOLLY** (*Comarostaphylis diversifolia*), page 112

> > **64b.** Leaves mostly less than 6 cm long.

> > > **66a.** Mature leaves commonly dark green above, with or without pubescence, shiny but not glossy; major veins may be yellowish green; on same plant, some leaves with spiny margins, some margins smooth; shrub oaks, widespread on dry slopes and canyons . . . . . . . . . . . . . . . . . . . . . . **SHRUB OAKS** (*Quercus* spp.), page 214
> > >
> > > **66b.** Leaves not as above in all ways; leaves tend to be glossy, glabrous at least above, always with more or less spiny margins.

> > > > **67a.** Leaves rounded or notched at tips, normally flat; scraped bark not noticeably aromatic; shrub, chaparral and pine forests.. **HOLLYLEAF REDBERRY** (*Rhamnus ilicifolia*), p. 224

**67b.** Leaves usually tapering to a point, sometimes abruptly, rarely rounded outline; leaf normally wavy (crisped); scraped bark aromatic with prussic acid odor; shrub or small tree, chaparral to oak woodlands. . . . . . . . **HOLLYLEAF CHERRY** . . . . . . . . . . . . . . . . . . . . . . . . . . . . . (*Prunus ilicifolia*), page 208

**62b.** Leaves not as above, margins lacking serration or serration not spiny, may be dentate (toothed); some leaves on a particular plant may have rather sharp serrations (e.g. *Rhus integrifolia*).

  **68a.** Mature trunks and branches with smooth red epidermis or somewhat furrowed, dark red brown to gray brown bark, bark often shredding; leaf margins lack serrations.

    **69a.** Mature leaves flat, base usually tapering abruptly to petiole, tip tapering gradually or abruptly to a point; widespread shrub. . . . . . . . . .
    . . . . . . . . . . . . . . . . . . . . . . **MANZANITA** (*Arctostaphylos* spp.), page 38

    **69b.** Mature leaves almost always somewhat cupped downward to nearly revolute, tapering gradually at both ends; shrub, chamise chaparral in western San Diego County and Baja California. . . . . . . . . . . . . .
    . . . . . . . . . . . . . . **MISSION-MANZANITA** (*Xylococcus bicolor*), page 310

  **68b.** Trunks and branches not as above; most leaves entire, some leaves serrate or dentate.

    **70a.** Leaves folded or curled upwards along midvein; rarely, leaves serrated.

      **71a.** Leaves green or green with reddish tint, thick and usually folded upward forming a narrow, shallow U or almost a V from the midvein; species found below 1800 m.

        **72a.** Twigs usually dark red; leaves sometimes with dark reddish tint, may be thin and flexible, somewhat aromatic when crushed; shrub, coastal sage scrub hills and washes below 600 m elevation. . . **LAUREL SUMAC** (*Malosma laurina*), page 192

        **72b.** Twigs tinted light reddish leaves mostly without reddish veins or margins, thick and leathery, not aromatic when crushed; shrub, dry chaparral between 300 and 1700 m. . . . .
        . . . . . . . . . . . . . . . . . . . . **SUGAR BUSH** (*Rhus ovata*), page 232

      **71b.** Leaves yellowish green, rust colored fuzz below; leaves thick, almost flat to slightly cupped upwards; shrub mostly high montane shrub above 1600 m in thickets on rocky ridges, conifer woodlands. . . **CHINQUAPIN** (*Chrysolepis sempervirens*), page 106

    **70b.** Leaves usually flat; sometimes cupped upward; rolled under, or crumpled; almost never folded upwards from the midvein as above; leaves may be dentate; some leaves entire, some serrated on same plant.

# VEGETATIVE KEY

**73a.** Leaves nearly same color on both surfaces, usually flat, at least not cupped upward.

**74a.** Leaves dark green to yellowish green, not fuzzy or pubescent, may be dentate.

**75a.** Leaves entire, lance-shaped to oblong or elliptical, dull yellowish green; shrub, dry chaparral slopes....... **BUSH POPPY (TREE POPPY)** (*Dendromecon rigida*), p. 116

**75b.** Leaves dentate, dark green, not lance shaped; shrub, coastal hills, inland to 900 m elevation. . . . . . . . . . . . . . . . . . . . . **CHAPARRAL BROOM** (*Baccharis pilularis*), page 64

**74b.** Leaves densely grayish, fuzzy on both surfaces; leaf margins crenate to coarsely dentate; mostly woody subshrub, dry gravelly and rocky places in chaparral to dry conifer and oak woodlands. . . . . . . . . . . . . . . . . . **THICKLEAF YERBA SANTA** . . . . . . . . . . . . . . . . . . . . . . . (*Eriodictyon crassifolium*), p. 136

**73b.** Leaves more or less bicolored, green or dark green above, paler below.

**76a.** Leaves mostly more than 3 cm long.

**77a.** Leaves flat to cupped upward in a U shape and smooth on both surfaces, though veins below sometimes prominent; most leaves entire, sometimes both entire and serrate on the same plant.

**78a.** Leaves commonly elliptic, margins irregularly toothed, somewhat aromatic when crushed, prominent midvein; shrub, ocean bluffs below 600 m.... **LEMONADEBERRY** (*Rhus intergrifolia*), page 230

**78b.** Leaves lance-shaped or oblong, margins entire, aromatic with strong odor of Bayleaf when crushed, midvein not especially prominent; tree or robust shrub, shaded slopes.. **CALIFORNIA BAY (LAUREL)** . . . . . . . . . . . . . . (*Umbellularia californica*), page 304

**77b.** Leaves not as above, midveins may be prominent, especially below.

**79a.** Mature leaves sticky or resinous, crumpled and uneven surface with prominent midvein; shrub, dry chaparral and conifer woodlands to the high desert. . . **YERBA SANTA** (*Eriodictyon trichocalyx*), page 138

**79b.** Leaves not sticky or resinous, veins curving to somewhat parallel with margin, prominent featherveining below; shrub, shaded hills and riparian areas, chaparral, oak and conifer forests. . . . . . . . . . . . . COFFEEBERRY (*Rhamnus californica*), page 220

**76b.** Leaves mostly less than 3 cm long, shade leaves sometimes longer (to 7 cm).

> **80a.** Leaves serrate at tips, smooth, more or less wedge-shaped at base; large gray barked shrub, dry chaparral and oak woodland slopes. . . . . . . . . . . . . . . . . . . . . . . . . . . . . .
> . . . . . . . . . . . . . . . . **WESTERN MOUNTAIN-MAHOGANY**
> . . . . . . . . . . . . . . . . . . . (*Cercocarpus betuloides*), page 100
>
> **80b.** Leaves, serrations (if present) usually involve most of leaf margins.

>> **81a.** Leaves similar in color on both surfaces; base of leaf has stipules (wart-like projecttions), usually prominent; leaves may be strongly revolute; widespread shrub. . . . . . . . . . . . . . **CALIFORNIA-LILACS**
>> . . . . . . . . . . . . . . . . . . . . . . (*Ceanothus* spp.), page 74
>>
>> **81b.** Leaves grayish green or whitish below, margins not serrated, stipules not prominent, leaves almost always strongly revolute; shrub or small tree, dry and rocky sage brush and conifer slopes above 1200 m.
>> . . . . . . . . . . . **CURLLEAF MOUNTAIN-MAHOGANY**
>> . . . . . . . . . . . . . . . . (*Cercocarpus ledifolius*), page 102

**LEAF TYPE V.** Leaves simple, alternate, mostly more than 10 mm wide, pinnately veined or with several veins with sparse branching arising from the base of long, narrow lance or linear-shaped leaves; mature leaves have more or less thin and flexible feel.

**82a.** Leaves whitish, pale green on both surfaces.

> **83a.** Leaves glaucous (covered with white film), often more than 5 cm long; common shrub or small tree, naturalized exotic, waste places and along roads. . . . . . . . . . . . . . . . . . . . **TREE TOBACCO** (*Nicotiana glauca*), page 196
>
> **83b.** Leaves scurfy, less than 5 cm long; shrub, near the coast, saline desert places, coastal sage scrub, and saltbrush communities. . . . . . . . . . . . . . . . .
> . . . . . . . . . . . . . . . . . . . **LENSCALE SALTBUSH** (*Atriplex lentiformis*), page 58

**82b.** Leaves not pale on both surfaces; green or dark green on upper or both surfaces, sometimes paler to yellowish or brownish below.

> **84a.** Leaves green, densely fuzzy on both surfaces, may be sticky, cause dermatitis in some people; subshrub, occasionally on dry disturbed places in chaparral and pine woodlands. . . . . . . . . . . . . . . . . . . . **POODLE-DOG BUSH**
> . . . . . . . . . . . . . . . . . . . . . . . . . . . . . . . . . . . . . . . . . . . (*Turricula parryi*), page 302
>
> **84b.** Leaves not as above.

>> **85a.** Leaves round in outline, without serration, with rusty fuzz below and on new growth; shrub, chaparral and oak woodland slopes. . . . . .
>> . . . . . . . . . . . . . . . . . . . . . . . . . . . . . . **STORAX** (*Styrax redivivus*), page 292

**85b.** Leaves lanceolate to ovate or elliptical to approximately linear, sometimes margins serrate or dentate, normally rusty fuzz below is absent.

**86a.** Leaves commonly approximately lance-shaped or oval to linear, few to several shallow dentations, same color on both surfaces.

**87a.** Leaves usually much longer than broad, lanceolate or oblanceolate to almost linear, usually serrated or with shallow dentations, may be glutinous or hairy; small stems not spine-tipped.

**88a.** Evergreen leaves, often with few to several shallow dentations above lower third of leaf; commonly, leaves and young stems glabrous, more or less glutinous, color about equal above and below; shrubs and subshrub, widely distributed... **BACCHARIS** (*Baccharis* spp.), p. 60

**88b.** Deciduous leaves, entire or with small serrations (edges may be rolled downward), usually somewhat darker above, leaves usually pubescent to hairy, not glutinous; shrub or small tree, common in wet places. . . . . .
. . . . . . . . . . . . . . . . . . . . . . **WILLOW** (*Salix* spp.), page 268

**87b.** Leaves mostly glabrous, usually somewhat longer than broad, lance shaped to ovate, mostly entire, sometimes with notch at tip; leaves and stems not glutinous; small stems spine-tipped; large shrub, coastal sage scrub and chaparral slopes below 900 m elevation. . . **GREENBARK CEANOTHUS**
. . . . . . . . . . . . . . . . . . . . . . . . . . . (*Ceanothus spinosus*), page 92

**86b.** Leaves elliptic or ovate to lance-shaped, lower surface paler to somewhat more yellowish green than upper surface.

**89a.** Leaves prominently feather-veined below, midvein and lateral veins easily felt.

**90a.** Leaf margins generally dentate or with coarse serrations on outer half of leaf.

**91a.** Leaf margins dentate, surfaces generally pubescent to villous; shrub, moist wooded slopes. . . . . . .
. . . . . . **CREAMBUSH** (*Holodiscus discolor*), page 158

**91b.** Leaf margins with relatively coarse serrations on outer half of leaf; leaves commonly glabrous above and pubescent below or pubescent on both sides; shrub or small tree, dry chaparral to oak woodlands. . . . . . . . **WESTERN MOUNTAIN-MAHOGANY**
. . . . . . . . . . . . . . . (*Cercocarpus betuloides*), page 100

**90b.** Leaf margins entire; serrations, if present, on entire leaf margin.

92a. Bark of young branchlets reddish; shrub, chaparral to conifer hillsides and ravines between 1200 and 2100 m. . . . . . . . . . . . . . . . . . . . . . **COFFEEBERRY** . . . . . . . . . . . . . . . . . (*Rhamnus californica*), page 220

92b. Bark of most branchlets whitish or yellowish to green or olive; widespread shrub. . . . . . . . . . . . . . . . . . . . **CALIFORNIA-LILACS** (*Ceanothus* spp.), page 74

89b. Leaves smooth on lower surface; except for midvein, lacking prominent easily felt veins.

93a. Leaves commonly roundish at least in outline to ovate or elliptical but may also approach lanceolate to oblong.

94a. Leaves with serrations or dentations, if present, confined to tips; flat, up to 4 cm long, 3 cm wide; shrub, dry conifer slopes. . . . . . . . . **SERVICE BERRY** . . . . . . . . . . . . . . . . (*Amelanchier utahensis*), page 34

94b. Leaves mostly with entire margins, folded upward from the midvein, usually greater than 5 cm long and 2-to 5-cm wide; shrub, dry chaparral and coastal sage slopes below 600 m. . **LAUREL SUMAC** . . . . . . . . . . . . . . . . . . . . (*Malosma laurina*), page 192

93b. Leaves lance-shaped, often tapering at both ends, usually more than 4 cm long.

95a. Leaves deciduous, light green and glabrous above and below.

96a. Young twigs pubescent to densely tomentose, becoming gray and furrowed, limited to wet places like stream banks; shrub or small tree, common in wet places. . . . . . . . . **WILLOW** . . . . . . . . . . . . . . . . . . . . . . (*Salix* spp.), page 268

96b. Young twigs not pubescent or tomentose, reddish to brown becoming dark brown or gray with smooth bark to gray and shreddy; not limited to wet places, but some species in moist woods.

97a. Young twigs brown, becoming gray with shreddy bark; leaves, obvious yellowish red midvein; shrub, moist woods or near streams. . . . . . . . . **WESTERN AZALEA** . . . . (*Rhododendron occidentale*), page 226

**97b**. Young twigs red brown to brown, becoming brown or gray with smooth bark; leaves without obvious midvein (likely to have taste of bitter almond); wide spread, along moist stream to desert slopes. . . . . . . . . **STONE FRUITS** (*Prunus* spp.), page 203

**95b**. Leaves evergreen, glossy to dark green above, paler to almost equal below, pubescent to hairy on leaf margins and/or veins, sometimes glaucous.

**98a**. Leaves entire, strong odor of bay when crushed; tree or robust shrub, shaded canyons and slopes, many communities. . . . . . . . . . . . . . . . . . . . . . . . . . . . . . . . . . . . . **CALIFORNIA BAY** . . . . . . . . . . (*Umbellularia californica*), page 304

**98b**. Leaves entire to slightly serrate, without strong odor of bay when crushed; large shrub, moist places in coastal sage scrub, chaparral, woodlands below 50 m. . . . . . . . . **WAXMYRTLE** . . . . . . . . . . . . . . (*Morella californica*), page 194

**LEAF TYPE VI.** Leaves alternate, mostly more than 10 mm wide, compound (that is, leaves divided into leaflets in a palmate or pinnate arrangement).

**99a**. Leaves with three or more leaflets; in a palmate pattern if four or more leaflets.

**100a**. Leaves with more than four leaflets in a palmate pattern, originating from same point and leaflets of same form; rounded subshrub, common after fire and occasional later below 1600 m, many plant communities. . . . . . . . . . . . . . . . . . . . . . . . . . . . . . . . . . . . . . . **LUPINE** (*Lupinus* spp.), page 186

**100b**. Leaves normally with three leaflets (sometimes with four or five) in various patterns with variously serrated margins.

**101a**. Leaflets with variously serrated margins.

**102a**. Stems with prickles; widespread shrub in woodlands and chaparral. . . **BLACKBERRY (RASPBERRY)** (*Rubus* spp.), page 260

**102b**. Stems without prickles.

**103a**. Leaflets joined at base; occasional sprawling shrub found in patches. . . . . . . . . . **SQUAW BUSH (BASKET SUMAC)** . . . . . . . . . . . . . . . . . . . . . . . . . . . . . (*Rhus aromatica*), page 228

**103b**. Leaflets separate at base; common sprawling shrub often in dense thickets, shaded chaparral and oak hillsides; causes dermititis in most people. . . . . . . . . . . . . **POISON-OAK** . . . . . . . . . . . . . . . . . . . . (*Toxicodendron diversilobum*), page 298

**101b.** Leaflets with entire margins.

> **104a.** Branchlets ending in stiff thorn; infrequent shrub, dry manzanita chaparral to live oak woodland slopes... **CHAPARRAL-PEA**
> .............................. (*Pickeringia montana*), page 200
> **104b.** Branchlets not ending in a stiff thorn.

>> **105a.** Leaves strongly ill-scented; shrub, coastal bluffs and deserts, coastal sage scrub to creosote bush communities. .
>> .............. **BLADDERPOD** (*Peritoma arborea*), page 198
>> **105b.** Leaves lacking strong smell.

>>> **106a.** Low subshrub, most upper stems green and rounded with strong tendency to be drought deciduous; dry coastal sage scrub and chaparral slopes...........
>>> .............. **DEERWEED** (*Acmispon glaber*), page 26
>>> **106b.** Erect shrub with green, angled branchlets; more or less drought deciduous leaves, pubescent at least below; exotic shrub, along highways and near the coast in waste places. **FRENCH BROOM** (*Genista monspessulana*), p. 152

**99b.** Leaves with five or more leaflets in a pinnate pattern, rarely three and then with sharp-toothed margins.

> **107a.** Leaflets holly-like, with sharp-toothed margins; shrub, shaded chaparral and dry oak to conifer slopes..... **BARBERRY** (*Berberis* spp.), page 70
> **107b.** Leaflets not holly-like, without sharp-toothed margins.

>> **108a.** Leaves or stems with thorns or prickles......... **FALSE-INDIGO**
>> .................................... (*Amorpha californica*), page 36
>> **108b.** Leaves and stems lacking thorns and prickles.

>>> **109a.** Leaflets 11 to 27, ranging from 3.5 to 7.5 cm long, edges serrated; tree or large shrub, locally common in oak woodlands. ...
>>> ...................... **WALNUT** (*Juglans californica*), page 160
>>> **109b.** Leaflets finely subdivided at least once into oval segments or lobes; leaves ranging from 3.5 to 8 cm long; small ill-smelling shrub, San Diego County in chaparral and coastal sage scrub. ...
>>> **SAN DIEGO MOUNTAIN MISERY** (*Chamaebatia australis*), p. 104

SQUAW BUSH (BASKET SUMAC), *Rhus aromatica*, page 228.

# SPECIES DESCRIPTIONS

The common names for the plants described herein are those in general usage. The latin names primarily follow those of ITIS, Integrated Taxonomic Information System (*www.itis.gov*). Plant descriptions are arranged in alphabetic order by genus. The descriptions emphasize vegetative features (rather than flower and fruiting characters) which are based on field observations and specimens filed at the Forest Fire laboratory, USDA Forest Service, Riverside; Botanic Garden, Rancho Santa Ana; Botanic Garden, Santa Barbara; and the Herbarium, University of California, Riverside.

Several manuals are available to help identify shrubs; *A Flora of Southern California* by Munz (1974) is the primary resource manual; Raven (1966) authored *Native Shrubs of Southern California*; and McMinn's (1939) text *An Illustrated Manual of California Shrubs,* remains a valuable, though dated, reference work. Other references include Abrams (1960), Collins (1974a,b), and Munz and Keck (1970). Smith (1976) authored a text on the flora of the Santa Barbara area. The latest flora for the entire state is *The Jepson Manual: Vascular Plants of California* (2012), which is updated online at *The Jepson eFlora* (*https://ucjeps.berkeley.edu/eflora*).

**Wildlife values** follow Martinet al. (1951), Van Dersal (1938), or USDA Forest Service (1969), and are defined for utilization of browse or fruits as preferred, staple, or low value. Cultural values are largely based upon information contained in literature discussing uses by Native Americans, especially the Cahuilla Indians of southern California (Balls 1972, Clarke 1977, Medsger 1966, Sweet 1962).

The section titled **Fire Response** provides information about the sprouting characteristics for each species, if known. Collectively, chaparral shrubs are well adapted to fire and have developed diverse methods of regeneration. Many species readily stump-sprout from trunks, main branches, enlarged basal burls, roots, or rhizomes. Species that do not sprout as so defined but are dependent solely upon seeds for regeneration are termed obligate seeders. Some dominant shrubs combine sprouting strategies; for example, chamise sprouts vigorously from basal burls and has a seedling response to fire as well.

Each species' **California distribution** is shown on the state map. Known, verified occurrence of a species in a particular county is shown in green. Data were provided by the Biota of North America Program (BONAP, *www.bonap.org*).

# *Acmispon glaber* (Vogel) L. Brouillet
## DEERWEED

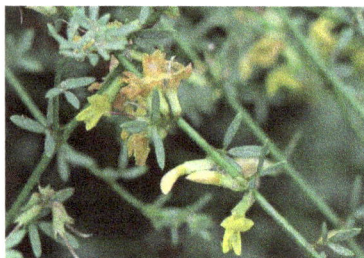

**PEA FAMILY** (Fabaceae)

**SYNONYM** *Lotus scoparius* (Nutt.) Ottley

**DESCRIPTION** Spreading, more or less drought-deciduous subshrub 0.5 to 1.2 m tall; long slender green branches become brown with age. **Leaves** 3-foliate with gland-like stipules at base of leaf, leaflets entire, lance- to oblanceolate-shaped, 3 to 10 mm (sometimes to 15 mm) long, 1 to 4 mm wide. **Flowers** January through May, 1- to 5-flowered clusters in leaf axils, 7 to 10 mm long, yellow or tinged with red. **Fruit** slightly curved pod.

**DISTRIBUTION** Common on dry slopes, below 1500 m (5000 ft); coastal sage scrub (soft chaparral) and chaparral.

**FIRE RESPONSE** Seedling response to fire; non-sprouter.

**WILDLIFE VALUE** Staple to low value browse for deer, livestock.

**CULTURAL VALUE** None known.

# *Acmispon glaber* (Vogel) L. Brouillet
## DEERWEED

# *Adenostoma fasciculatum* Hook. & Arn.
## CHAMISE (GREASEWOOD)

**ROSE FAMILY** (Rosaceae)

**DESCRIPTION** Diffusely branched, evergreen shrub, 0.5 to 3.5 m tall, reddish bark becoming shreddy with age. **Leaves** green, mostly 4 to 14 leaf, alternate bundles crowded on stems, rarely single, linear, 4 to 10 (> 20) mm long, sharp-pointed, usually channeled on one side; seedling leaves divided one, two, or three times into two to several linear lobes. **Flowers** February through June, small, white, compact clusters 4 to 12 cm long. **Fruit**, achene enclosed by hardened floral tube.

**DISTRIBUTION** Common dominant on dry slopes below 1500 m (5000 ft); chaparral merging into coastal sage scrub (soft chaparral) and desert chaparral; Channel Islands, coast ranges, Humboldt County to Baja California, Sierra Nevada foothills. Var. *obtusifolium* S. Wats., broader leaves, almost obtuse; shorter (3-7 mm long, 1+ mm wide); Los Angeles County southward.

**FIRE RESPONSE** Stump-sprouts from basal burls and lateral shoots after fire; many seeds germinate after some fires, only few survive.

**WILDLIFE VALUE** Readily browsed few years after fire; cover for deer.

**CULTURAL VALUE** Native Americans used infusion of bark and leaves as cure for syphilis, and oil of plant to cure skin infections (Sweet 1962); scale insect on plant used to bind arrows, baskets, etc.

# *Adenostoma fasciculatum* Hook. & Arn.
## CHAMISE (GREASEWOOD)

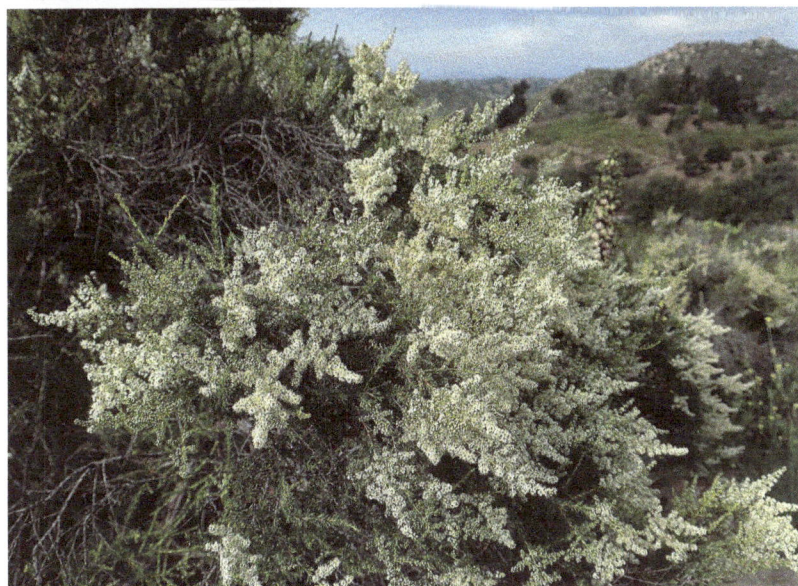

# *Adenostoma sparsifolium* Torr.
## RED SHANK (RIBBON BUSH)

**ROSE FAMILY** (Rosaceae)

**DESCRIPTION** Evergreen shrub or small tree, 2 to 6 m tall, red brown bark; peels in thin sheets and strips; twigs yellowish green, resinous, sticky. **Leaves** linear, alternate, 4 to 10 (< 15) mm long, leaves not in bundles, often crowded on young twigs; shoots arise from leaf axil buds with leaf persisting. **Flowers** July and August, white or pinkish, fragrant, loose clusters 2 to 6 cm long. **Fruit**, achene enclosed by hardened floral tube.

**DISTRIBUTION** Discrete, disjunct populations, dry slopes, mesas below 1800 m (6000 ft); chaparral, often dominant in Baja California, Mexico; red shank-dominated communities common in southern Riverside and northern San Diego counties; small enclave on Los Angeles-Ventura County border; disjunct communities in northern Santa Barbara County into San Luis Obispo County (Hanes 1965).

**FIRE RESPONSE** Stump-sprouts from basal burls; seed response to fire.

**WILDLIFE VALUE** Low value; cover for deer.

**CULTURAL VALUE** Leaves, same as *A. fasciculatum;* ground into powder, mixed with grease for salve.

# *Adenostoma sparsifolium* Torr.
## RED SHANK (RIBBON BUSH)

# *Adolphia californica* S. Wats.
## ADOLPHIA

**BUCKTHORN FAMILY** (Rhamnaceae)

**DESCRIPTION** Shrub, thorny, stiff, many-branched, drought-deciduous; to 1 m tall; branches green. **Leaves** round to oval, opposite, 2 to 5 mm long; 2 to 3 mm wide, fall early, pale green, about 5 mm long or more. **Flowers** December through April, inconspicuous, greenish white, five petals. **Fruit**, 3-lobed capsule 4 to 5 mm wide.

**DISTRIBUTION** Dry flats and canyons; uncommon.

**FIRE RESPONSE** Obligate seeder.

**WILDLIFE VALUE** Low value.

**CULTURAL VALUE** Unknown.

# *Adolphia californica* S. Wats.
## ADOLPHIA

# *Amelanchier utahensis* Koehne
## SERVICE-BERRY

**ROSE FAMILY** (Rosaceae)

**DESCRIPTION** Deciduous shrub, much branched, 1 to 5 m tall; youngest twigs reddish, mature with ash-gray bark, rigid twigs, white pubescence on young growth. **Mature leaves** gray green, color nearly equal above and to somewhat lighter below, alternate, roundish to oval or elliptic, usually flat, 1 to 4 cm long, 0.5 to 3 cm wide, usually tomentose to some degree to near base on both sides, toothed or serrate especially on outer two-thirds of leaf margin, sometimes serrations restricted to end of leaf, rarely entire, leaves on petioles 5 to 15 mm long, rather delicate midvein most prominent near base, 11 to 13 pairs of lateral veins, tend to thin and flex. **Flowers** April through May, white, 3 to 6 flower clusters, five petals, deciduous. **Fruit** 6 to 10 mm diameter, purplish black, juicy to dry.

**DISTRIBUTION** Dry slopes 900 to 2100 m (3000–7000 ft); ponderosa pine, Jeffrey pine, pinyon-juniper, western juniper; San Bernardino, San Gabriel Mountains.

**FIRE RESPONSE** Stump-sprouter after fire.

**WILDLIFE VALUE** Staple browse for deer, livestock; fruits preferred by birds and many mammals.

**CULTURAL VALUE** Native American, berries eaten fresh or dried; pounded, stored for later use as 4.5 to 7 kg (10–15 lb) loaves; green inner bark, boiled for eyewash (Clarke 1977).

# *Amelanchier utahensis* Koehne
## SERVICE-BERRY

# *Amorpha californica* Nutt.
## FALSE-INDIGO

**PEA FAMILY** (Fabaceae)

**DESCRIPTION** Slender, deciduous shrub, 1.5 to 3 m tall, somewhat hairy twigs; young stems green, soon become brownish then dark gray; prickly-like glands on branchlets and leaf midveins. **Leaves** darker green above; gland dotted below; mature leaves 0.8 to 2 cm long, 11 to 27 leaflets, usually oblong-elliptic with entire margins, mature leaflets 1 to 3 cm long, 0.5 to 2 cm wide; leaflets opposite or nearly so, give appearance of 7 to 13 pairs along leaf petiole, on short (1-2 mm) leaflet petiole. **Flowers** April to July, crowded spike. **Fruit**, purplish pods, 6 to 8 mm long.

**SIMILAR SPECIES** If lacking prickly glands, probably desert false indigo (*A. fruticosa* L.)

**DISTRIBUTION** Dry wooded or brushy slopes, below 2300 m (7500 ft); ponderosa/Jeffrey pine communities and chaparral; Santa Rosa, Santa Ana Mountains to Santa Lucia Mountains, San Gabriel, San Bernardino, San Jacinto Mountains.

**FIRE RESPONSE** Stump-sprouts readily after fire.

**WILDLIFE VALUE** Deer and sheep browse leaves.

**CULTURAL VALUE** Unknown.

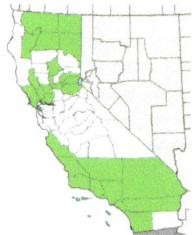

# *Amorpha californica* Nutt.
## FALSE-INDIGO

# *Arctostaphylos* spp.
## MANZANITAS

**EASTWOOD MANZANITA** (*Arctostaphylos glandulosa*)

**HEATHER FAMILY** (Ericaceae)

**DESCRIPTION** Manzanitas (Spanish for "little apples"), evergreen shrubs or small trees with stiff branches and dark reddish-brown bark. **Leaves** alternate and simple. **Flowers** urn or bell-shaped. The Jepson eflora reports 61 species in the California flora, 7 more common of which are covered by this guide. Species differ in fire response mechanisms. **Eastwood manzanita** is only mainland species in this guide that has a basal burl, therefore, often vigorously resprouts after fire. One Channel Island species [**woollyleaf manzanita**, *A. tomentosa* (Pursh) Lindl.] also forms a burl. Other species depend primarily in seedlings for post-fire recovery.

**WILDLIFE VALUE** Low value browse, new growth eaten by deer; if heavily used, indicate range problems; berries, staple of many animals including fox, raccoon, skunk, coyote, quail, bear.

**CULTURAL VALUE** Native American, very valuable for food, medicine, shelter, pleasure (Sweet 1962). Pulp of berries soaked in water for tart beverage; seeds ground into meal. Leaves mixed with tobacco or steeped in water for tea to relieve diarrhea or wash poison oak rash (Clarke 1977).

**EASTWOOD MANZANITA** (*Arctostaphylos glandulosa*)

*Key to Manzanitas*

**1a.** Root crown burl present, (detected as swollen collar near ground surface in zone between above-ground stems and roots); leaves oblong, somewhat mucronate, dull green, hairy; sometimes sticky; in chaparral, conifer woodlands, or forests. . . . . . . . . . . . . . . . . . . . . . . . . . **EASTWOOD MANZANITA** *A. glandulosa*

**1b.** Root crown burl not present.

> **2a.** Leaves usually oblong to oval, sometimes obovate; tip usually mucronate.

>> **3a.** Leaves usually glaucous or waxy in appearance; locally common shrub; on dry chaparral slopes. . . . **BIGBERRY MANZANITA,** *A. glauca*

>> **3b.** Leaves not glaucous or waxy appearing.

>>> **4a.** Majority of petioles have appearance of being at right angle with stem; young stems, dense glandular pubescence or villous (do not appear shiny green); dry chaparral, pine woodland slopes, San Bernardino Mountains to Baja California. . . . . . . . . . . . . . . . . . . . .
. . . . . . . . **PINK-BRACTED MANZANITA,** *A. pringlei* ssp. *drupacea*

>>> **4b.** Petioles not commonly appear at right angles with stem, young stems glabrous to finely glandular pubescent or pubescent (usually appear shiny green); dry chaparral to conifer woodland slopes, Santa Rosa, San Gabriel Mountains, north to Tehachapi Mountains. . . . . . . . . . . . . . . . . . . . . . . **PARRY MANZANITA,** *A. parryana*

> **2b.** Leaves mostly elliptic; commonly, tips gradually narrow to a point; rarely mucronate.

>> **5a.** Leaves green, more or less shiny, usually hairless; leaf venation usually impressive to eye; dry, transmontane slopes in chaparral, oak, and conifer communities. . . . . . . . . . . **MEXICAN MANZANITA,** *A. pungens*

>> **5b.** Leaves green to yellowish green, not particularly shiny, usually more or less pubescent; venation less impressive than above; dry chaparral, San Diego County. . . . . . . . . . . . . . . . . . **OTAY MANZANITA,** *A. otayensis*

# *Arctostaphylos glandulosa* Eastw.
## EASTWOOD MANZANITA (CROWN MANZANITA)

**HEATHER FAMILY** (Ericaceae)

**DESCRIPTION** Evergreen spreading shrub with basal burl, 1.5 to 2.5 m tall; smooth reddish stems, coarse hairy, greenish, glandular branchlets; glandular sheath shed with maturity leaving red bark-covered stems (only ssp. *glandulosa* has glandular branchlets); mature leaves stiff and leathery, elliptic-ovate or lanceolate, margins entire. **Leaves** dull green or yellowish, pointed at tips, more or less glandular-pubescent on leaf margins and both surfaces, becoming glabrate with age but retains somewhat rough feel, 3 to 6 cm long, 1 to 4 cm wide, mature leaves nearly flat, petiole 5 to 12 mm long, seedling leaves same shape but dentate margin. **Flowers** February to May, white bloom subtended by sticky, lance-shaped, persistent pubescent bracts. **Fruit**, berry-like, about 8 mm across, green glandular and sticky when immature, eventually reddish brown and less sticky, glandular (only ssp. *glandulosa,* glandular fruit).

**DISTRIBUTION** Common shrub, 300 to 1800 m (1000–6000 ft); chaparral, mixed conifer to ponderosa and Jeffrey pines; coast ranges, to Cuyamaca Mountains, San Diego County.

**FIRE RESPONSE** Stump sprouts from enlarged burls after fire or cutting.

**WILDLIFE VALUE** Poor browse, berries desired.

**CULTURAL VALUE** See genus.

# *Arctostaphylos glandulosa* Eastw.
## EASTWOOD MANZANITA (CROWN MANZANITA)

# *Arctostaphylos glauca* Lindl.
## BIGBERRY MANZANITA

**HEATHER FAMILY** (Ericaceae)

**DESCRIPTION** Evergreen, erect shrub or small tree without basal burl, 2 to 4 (to 6 m) tall, smooth red-brown mature bark and/or waxy appearing green to pale green, hairless to finely pubescent young twigs; old bark more or less continually shed. **Leaves** somewhat glaucous, gray green, stiff, leathery, flat, ovate to oblong, rounded to tapering at apex, 2.5 to 4.5 cm long, 1 to 3 cm wide, petioles 6 to 12 mm long. **Flowers** December to March, white to pinkish, urn-shaped, about 8 to 9 mm long. Young **fruit**, sticky glandular berry, 12 to 15 mm diameter.

**DISTRIBUTION** Common on dry slopes below 1400 m (4500 ft); chaparral; mountains, southern California northward to Mt. Hamilton, Mt. Diablo, south to Baja California.

**FIRE RESPONSE** Non-sprouter, obligate seeder after fire.

**WILDLIFE VALUE** See genus.

**CULTURAL VALUE** See above for genus. Native Americans, especially desired for large fruit.

# *Arctostaphylos otayensis* Wies. & Schreib.
## OTAY MANZANITA

**HEATHER FAMILY** (Ericaceae)

**DESCRIPTION** Erect evergreen shrub, to 2.5 m tall, without basal burl, reddish to red-brown mature stems; young stems hairy, sometimes with few glandular hairs. Mature **leaves** stiff and leathery, elliptical to ovate, rarely with mucronate tip, 1 to 4.5 cm long, 0.6 to 2.5 cm wide; petioles, 2 to 10 mm long, pubescent, leaves slightly to densely pubescent or glandular pubescent, grayish green to green both sides, sometimes darker above. **Flowers** February to April, white to rose, urn-shaped, 3 to 6 mm long, subtended by leafy bracts, in open panicles or racemes. **Fruit**, round berry becoming pale brown or red, 3 to 5 mm across, contains solid nut.

**DISTRIBUTION** Dry slopes, 550 to 1500 m (1800–5000 ft); chaparral; San Diego Mountains, especially Laguna Mountains.

**FIRE RESPONSE** Non-sprouter; apparently obligated to regenerate by seedlings after fire.

**WILDLIFE VALUE** See genus.

**CULTURAL VALUE** See genus.

44

# *Arctostaphylos otayensis* Wies. & Schreib.
## OTAY MANZANITA

# *Arctostaphylos parryana* Lemmon
## PARRY MANZANITA

**HEATHER FAMILY** (Ericaceae)

**DESCRIPTION** Evergreen, diffusely spreading shrub without basal burl, 1 to 2 m tall, without enlarged root-crown, bark on main stems reddish brown; lateral branches lie on ground, sometimes root on contact; branchlets and petioles canescent to glabrous, not glandular. Stiff, leathery **leaves**, bright green, somewhat shiny, darker above, hairless, ovate, elliptic or broadly oval, entire margins, flat, rounded or acute to a point at apex, 2 to 4.5 cm long, 1 to 3 cm wide, on petioles 5 to 10 mm long. **Flowers** February to April, white, urn-shaped, 6 to 7 mm long, few-flowered clusters. **Fruit**, dark red berry, 5 to 12 mm, hairless, nutlets usually separable, sometimes fused.

**DISTRIBUTION** Dry slopes, 1200 to 2300 m (4000–7500 ft); chaparral, ponderosa and Jeffrey pine to mixed conifer; Santa Rosa Mountains to San Gabriel Mountains, Mt. Pinos area to Tehachapi Mountains.

**FIRE RESPONSE** Non-sprouter after fire, cutting; roots from lateral branches on ground; obligate seeder after fire.

**WILDLIFE VALUE** See genus.

**CULTURAL VALUE** See genus.

# *Arctostaphylos parryana* Lemmon
## PARRY MANZANITA

**PARRY MANZANITA** (*Arctostaphylos parryana*)

**SIMILAR SPECIES** *Arctostaphylos patula* Greene (right), glandular-pubescent branchlets, petioles, infloresence; dry slopes, 1500 to 2700 m (5000-9000 ft); in ponderosa and Jeffrey pine to mixed conifers, Santa Rosa Mountains to San Gabriel Mountains.

# *Arctostaphylos pringlei* Parry
## PINK-BRACTED MANZANITA

**HEATHER FAMILY** (Ericaceae)

**DESCRIPTION** Evergreen, erect shrub, without basal burl, 2 to 4 m tall, smooth reddish brown shedding bark, young stems greenish becoming red, densely hairy glandular branchlets. **Leaves** stiff and leathery, 2.5 to 5.5 cm long, 1.5 to 3 cm wide, ovate-roundish, gray green, fine hairs, rough to touch on both sides; petioles 5 to 7 mm long. **Flowers** February to June, rose colored, urn-shaped, 7 to 8 mm long, subtended by lance-shaped deciduous pink bracts, 5 to 6 mm long. **Fruit,** round berry 6 to 10 mm across, glandular, hairy, becoming red. Subspecies *drupacea* (Parry) P.V. Wells restricted to California.

**DISTRIBUTION** Dry slopes, 1400 to 2300 m (4500–7500 ft); chaparral, ponderosa and Jeffrey pine; San Bernardino San Jacinto Mountains to Baja California.

**FIRE RESPONSE** Non-sprouter; obligate seeder after fire.

**WILDLIFE VALUE** See genus.

**CULTURAL VALUE** See genus.

48

# *Arctostaphylos pungens* Kunth
## MEXICAN MANZANITA

**HEATHER FAMILY** (Ericaceae)

**DESCRIPTION** Erect evergreen shrub without basal burl, 2 to 3 m tall, smooth red brown bark, grayish with age, finely hairy twigs. **Leaves** bright green, shinier above, hairless, elliptic or obovate, 1.5 to 4 cm long, 1 to 2 cm wide, petioles 3 to 10 mm long. **Flowers** January to March, white, urn-shaped, 6 mm long. **Fruit** brown ± hairless berries, separate or irregularly united nutlets ridged at back.

**DISTRIBUTION** Dry transmontane slopes, 900 to 2100 m (3000–7000 ft); chaparral, ponderosa and Jeffrey pine to canyon live oak woodlands and forests; common in San Diego County, San Gabriel, San Bernardino, San Jacinto Mountains.

**FIRE RESPONSE** Non-sprouter, without basal burl; roots from branches; obligate seeder after fire.

**WILDLIFE VALUE** See genus.

**CULTURAL VALUE** See genus.

# *Artemisia californica* Less.
## COAST SAGEBRUSH

**SUNFLOWER FAMILY** (Asteraceae)

**DESCRIPTION** Grayish, mostly woody subshrub, 0.5 to 1.5 m tall, evergreen, sage-like odor; young stems, white to yellowish, gray with age; old bark, shreddy. **Leaves** and young stems, woolly. **Leaves** alternate, numerous, dense short leafy branches, divided mostly once or twice into segments, at least upper ones commonly linear and borne in fascicles, 1 to 6.5 cm long, mostly 1 mm or less wide; seedling leaves with shorter and broader segments, 1 to 2 cm long, to 2 mm wide. **Flowers** August to December, clusters with many nodding heads, 3 to 5 mm wide. **Fruit**, achene.

**DISTRIBUTION** Common, exposed slopes, hills, below 900 m (3000 ft).

**FIRE RESPONSE** Non-sprouter, exhibits vigorous seedling response after fire.

**WILDLIFE VALUE** Low value browse.

**CULTURAL VALUE** Cahuilla Indians, products used to prepare young girls for womanhood; important medicinal plant (Clarke 1977); may have been dried and smoked with tobacco.

# *Artemisia tridentata* Nutt.
## BASIN (BIG) SAGEBRUSH

**SUNFLOWER FAMILY** (Asteraceae)

**DESCRIPTION** Evergreen shrub, 0.5 to 3 m tall, short trunk; young stems tend to be yellowish to yellowish green, become gray and shreddy with age. Simple **leaves**, opposite and clustered, grayish, spatulate, canescent or pubescent, 1 to 4 cm long, to 8 mm wide, 3-toothed (rarely 4 to 9) at apex, strong sagebrush smell. **Flowers** July to November, narrow clusters, spike or panicle of many small heads persisting after fruiting. **Fruit**, achene.

**DISTRIBUTION** Dry slopes and plains, 450 to 3200 m (1500–10,600 ft); sagebrush, ponderosa pine, Jeffrey pine, western juniper, and pinyon-juniper; Laguna Mountains, San Diego County, western edge of deserts to Sierra Nevada.

**FIRE RESPONSE** Fibrous root system, occasionally root-sprouting after fire, cutting; indicator of deep soils.

**WILDLIFE VALUE** Staple when eaten with other forage, decreases amount of essential oils in sagebrush which act as rumen flora inhibitors.

**CULTURAL VALUE** Cahuilla Indians, source of medicine and food (Clarke 1977).

# *Atriplex canescens* (Pursh) Nutt.
## WINGSCALE SALTBUSH (SHADSCALE)

**AMARANTH FAMILY** (Amaranthaceae)

**DESCRIPTION** Evergreen, erect, stiff-branched dioecious shrub, 0.4 to 2 m tall, gray scaly or scurfy branches, young branchlets, yellowish green, become yellow gray with age. **Leaves** alternate, often crowded in bunches, not fasicled, linear-spatulate or narrowly oblong, margins entire, 1 to 5 cm long, 2 to 8 mm wide, often somewhat rolled under (not revolute), gray to olive colored, slightly darker above with dense scurf (scales) on both sides, curled under at edges. **Male and female flowers** July to August, separate plants, clusters arise from leaf axils, floral racemes become more leafy toward base. **Fruits** 4-winged utricles, single seed, wings entire or dentate.

**DISTRIBUTION** Dry slopes, flats, washes, below 2200 m (7000 ft); saltbush, creosote, pinyon-juniper and subsaline sinks; deserts.

**FIRE RESPONSE** Fire resistant; non-sprouter, taproot deep, to 9 to 12 m (30–40 ft).

**WILDLIFE VALUE** Fruits, preferred food by birds, rodents; staple browse for wildlife and livestock, concentrated feeding may cause scours in livestock.

**CULTURAL VALUE** Native Americans, ground seed for meal and emetic; saliva moistened, ground roots or flowers to sooth ant bites; ashes stirred into water changed color of meal to greenish blue (Sweet 1962).

# *Atriplex lentiformis* (Torr.) S. Wats.
## LENSCALE SALTBUSH

**AMARANTH FAMILY** (Amaranthaceae)

**DESCRIPTION** Wide-spreading leafy dioecious shrub, 1 to 3 m tall, often wider than tall; young twigs yellowish brown becoming grayish brown. **Leaves** alternate, triangular or ovate, truncate to wedge-shaped at base, blunt point, deciduous in desert forms, tend to be evergreen elsewhere, 1.0 to 5 cm long, 0.5 to 4 cm wide, 1-veined from base, sessile or on short petiole, grayish, fine-scaly surface. Tiny **Flowers** August to October, long clusters. **Fruit**, bracts flattish or convex, 3 to 7 mm long.

**DISTRIBUTION** Along coast, in desert, saline places mostly from 500 m (1600 ft) and below; in coastal sage scrub (soft chaparral) and saltbush.

**FIRE RESPONSE** Somewhat fire resistant foliage; profuse seeder.

**WILDLIFE VALUE** Preferred browse of mule deer, livestock; seeds important to many animals.

**CULTURAL VALUE** Probably same as for **wingscale saltbush** (*A. canescens*).

# *Atriplex lentiformis* (Torr.) S. Wats.
## LENSCALE SALTBUSH

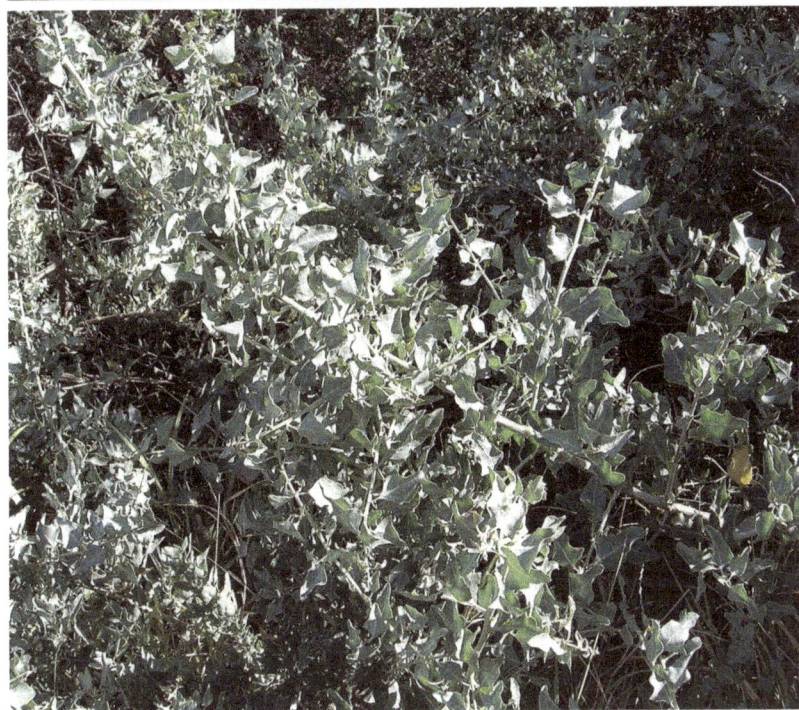

# *Baccharis* spp.
## FALSE WILLOW

**BROOM BACCHARIS** (*Baccharis sarothroides*)

(Asteraceae)

*Key to Baccharis*

1a. Leaves lance shaped to linear.

    1b. Leaves linear, up to 2 cm long, not glutinous or slightly so; branches somewhat resinous, often nearly leafless; shrub on sandy washes usually near water courses, coastal sage, and creosote bush scrub. . . . . . . . . . . . . . .

    . . . . . . . . . . . . . . . . . . . . . . . . . . . . . . . **BROOM BACCHARIS**, *B. sarothroides*

    1b. Leaves lance shaped, mature leaves more than 2 cm long, usually somewhat glutinous, stems leafy and not resinous; shrub, common along streams and other moist ground below 900 m, associated with coastal sage scrub and chaparral. . . . . . . . **MULEFAT (STICKY BACCHARIS)**, *B. glutinosa*

1a. Leaves somewhat wedge shaped in outline; shrub, common on coastal strand, coastal sage scrub, below 900 m elevation. . . . . . . . . . . . . . . . . . . . . . . . . . .

    . . . . . . . . . . . . . . . . . . . . . . . . . . . . . . . . . . . . **CHAPARRAL BROOM**, *B. pilularis*

**MULEFAT** (*Baccharis glutinosa*)

# *Baccharis glutinosa* Pers.
## MULEFAT (STICKY BACCHARIS, SEEP-WILLOW)

**SUNFLOWER FAMILY** (Asteraceae)

**DESCRIPTION** Willow-like evergreen shrub, 1 to 3 m tall; slender, straight, relatively unbranched stems; young stems somewhat herbaceous and greenish to reddish, may be pubescent, become yellowish to brown with age. Light green shiny **leaves**, color equal above and below, commonly glutinous, small pits on underside of leaves, alternate leaves lance-shaped, willowlike, 5 to 15 cm long, 7 to 22 mm wide, sessile or on short petiole (to 2 mm), tapering at both ends with some serration above middle or entire, single midvein or with long lateral veins arising from near base of midvein, soon becoming parallel. **Flowers** most of year, terminal clusters, numerous, bracts on flower heads, 4 mm long, 3 to 4 series of straw-colored bracts. **Fruit**, small ribbed achene.

**DISTRIBUTION** Along streams, moist ground, to 900 m (3000 ft).

**FIRE RESPONSE** Stump-sprouts after fire, cutting.

**WILDLIFE VALUE** Low-value browse plant.

**CULTURAL VALUE** Unknown.

# *Baccharis pilularis* DC.
## CHAPARRAL BROOM

**SUNFLOWER FAMILY** (Asteraceae)

**DESCRIPTION** Erect, much-branched evergreen shrub, straight green branchlets become brown with age, 1 to 4 m tall. **Leaves** alternate, numerous, somewhat wedge-shaped, dark green, may be darker above, 1.0 to 4 cm long, 5 to 15 mm wide, or more, somewhat 3-veined from the base, irregularly toothed (dentate) margins above lower one-third, teeth few to 6 or 7 points or sometimes entire. **Flowers** August to December, numerous heads on branchlets, brownish white, may make plant appear woolly. **Fruit**, small ribbed achene.

**SIMILAR SPECIES** **Plummer Baccharis** (*B. plummerae* Gray), with hairy-sticky leaves.

**DISTRIBUTION** Common along coastal hills and inland, to 900 m (3000 ft); coastal strand, coastal sage scrub (soft chaparral), chamise chaparral.

**FIRE RESPONSE** Colony forming, recommended for dune fixation; presumably root-sprouter after fire.

**WILDLIFE VALUE** Staple browse for mule deer; seeds eaten by quail, etc.

**CULTURAL VALUE** None known.

# *Baccharis sarothroides* Gray
## BROOM BACCHARIS

**SUNFLOWER FAMILY** (Asteraceae)

**DESCRIPTION** Erect shrub, 2 to 4 m tall, with grooved broom-like, green, somewhat resinous stems, branchlets becoming reddish with gray-textured bark, stems nearly leafless below. **Leaves** alternate, approximately linear, rigid, entire, 0.6 to 2 cm long, 1 to 2 mm wide. **Flowers** June to October, heads 5 to 8 mm long, cream colored or brownish. **Fruit**, ribbed achene.

**DISTRIBUTION** Sandy washes or soils, mostly below 300 m (1000 ft); coastal sage scrub (soft chaparral) to creosotebush.

**FIRE RESPONSE** Unknown.

**WILDLIFE VALUE** Unknown.

**CULTURAL VALUE** Unknown.

# *Baccharis sarothroides* Gray
## BROOM BACCHARIS

# *Bahiopsis laciniata* (A. Gray) E.E. Schill. & Panero
## SAN DIEGO SUNFLOWER

**SUNFLOWER FAMILY** (Asteraceae)

**SYNONYM** *Viguiera laciniata* A. Gray

**DESCRIPTION** Rounded subshrub, 1 to 2 m tall, more or less resinous with tough feeling surfaces, much-branched, slender rough pubescent and more or less brittle stems, young stems greenish, bark becoming brown with age. **Leaves** simple, at least lower ones opposite, 2 to 5 cm long, to 1.5 cm wide, lance-shaped, often with an abrupt base, margins serrated, thick and leathery, darker green above with sparse short, sometimes recurved hairs especially on veins. **Flowers** February to June, blooms in heads with 8 to 13 rays, 10 to 15 mm long, many tube flowers. **Fruit**, laterally commressed achene.

**DISTRIBUTION** Dry slopes, to 800 m (2500 ft); chamise chaparral, coastal sage scrub (soft chaparral).

**FIRE RESPONSE** Unknown.

**WILDLIFE VALUE** Low value browse.

**CULTURAL VALUE** None known.

# *Bahiopsis laciniata* (A. Gray) E.E. Schill. & Panero
## SAN DIEGO SUNFLOWER

# *Berberis dictyota* Jepson
## BARBERRY

**BARBERRY FAMILY** (Berberidaceae)

**SYNONYM** *Mahonia dictyota* (Jepson) Fedde

**DESCRIPTION** Evergreen shrub with erect stems, few branched, to 1.8 m tall. **Leaves** alternate, compound, divided into five (rarely 3 or 7) holly-like leaflets, 3 to 5 cm long and 1.5 to 3 cm wide, green above, paler and white-filmy below, with prominent midvein, margins wavy with stiff spines. **Leaves** on petiole to 1 cm long. **Flowers** February through May, yellow in drooping racemes. **Fruit**, berry 6 to 7 mm long, blue black or filmy.

**SIMILAR SPECIES** If leaves are large oval shaped, glossy-green on both surfaces or somewhat darker above with up to nine leaflets, terminal leaflet to 8 cm long, 5 cm wide, it is **shiny-leaf Barberry** (*Berberis pinnata* Lag.). If leaflets lance-shaped, terminal leaflets mostly less than 4 cm long, 1 cm wide, all less than 2 cm wide, it is the rare *Berberis nevinii* A. Gray.

**DISTRIBUTION** Local, dry rocky foothills, 600 to 1800 m (2000–6000 ft); chaparral and oak to ponderosa and Jeffrey pine communities.

**FIRE RESPONSE** Suckers, root-sprouts after fire.

**WILDLIFE VALUE** Low value browse and fruits.

**CULTURAL VALUE** Important medicinal source for ulcers, served as tonic and flavoring for soup, etc. (Sweet 1962).

# *Berberis dictyota* Jepson
## BARBERRY

# *Brickellia californica* (Torr. & Gray) Gray
## BRICKELLBUSH

**SUNFLOWER FAMILY** (Asteraceae)

**DESCRIPTION** Rounded, aromatic subshrub, with many stems from woody base young stems pubescent, light brown, becoming darker. **Leaves** alternate, pubescent, deltoid to ovate, sometimes taper to blunt point, with rounded serrations, rarely heart-shaped at base, 1 to 4 cm long, petiole 1 to 5 mm long. **Flowers** June to November, cream-colored heads on pedicels, arise from leaf axils and in small, terminal clusters, somewhat leafy. **Fruit**, ribbed achene.

**DISTRIBUTION** Washes, dry slopes, below 2100 m (7000 ft); coastal sage scrub (soft chaparral), chamise; Sierra Nevada foothills.

**FIRE RESPONSE** Believed to be non-sprouter or poor sprouter after fire.

**WILDLIFE VALUE** Low value or staple browse.

**CULTURAL VALUE** Unknown.

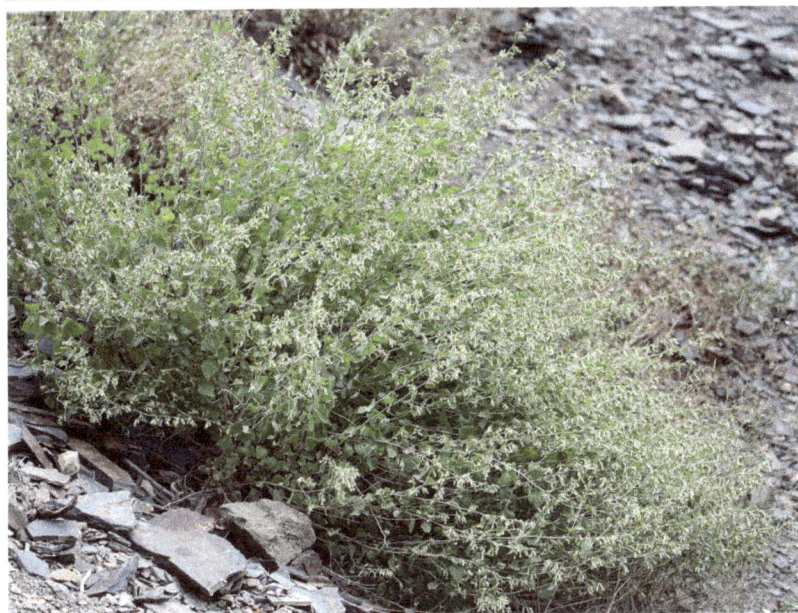

# *Ceanothus* spp.
## CALIFORNIA-LILACS

**BUCKBRUSH** (*Ceanothus cuneatus*)

**BUCKBRUSH FAMILY** (Rhamnaceae)

**DESCRIPTION** Shrubs or small trees, mostly evergreen, in southern California. **Leaves** simple, alternate or opposite, deciduous or evergreen. **Flowers** small, five-parted, spoon-shaped petals, glandular disk. **Fruit**, 3-lobed capsule; when viewed from top, bears mark similar to Mercedes Benz insignia. Of ca. 60 species in the genus, 40 native to California, 17 to southern California.

**WILDLIFE VALUE** Most species preferred for browse by deer, bighorn sheep.

**CULTURAL VALUE** Southern California species seem not to have been heavily used; available information suggesting its use is limited. Flowers of several species can be used as substitute for soap.

*Key to Ceanothus*

**1a**. Leaves opposite.

> **2a**. Leaves usually flat, spatulate to obovate, sometimes notched at apex, smooth margins; common on dry chaparral and conifer woodland slopes below 1800 m. . . . . . . . . . . . . . . . . . . . . . . . . . . . . **BUCKBRUSH**, *C. cuneatus*
>
> **2b**. Leaves mostly cupped upwards or rolled downward at edges.
>
> > **3a**. Leaves commonly rolled downward, never cupped upward, dull green above, distinctly white-tomentose below, vaguely oak appearing leaf; common in chaparral below 1100 m. . . . . . . . . . . . . . . . . . . . . . . . .
> > . . . . . . . . . . . . . . . . . . . . . . . **HOARYLEAF CEANOTHUS**, *C. crassifolius*
> >
> > **3b**. Leaves commonly cupped upwards, usually pubescent below, sometimes tomentose on both sides, rarely rolled downward, grayish green to yellowish green above, gray below; locally common in chaparral, sagebrush, and pine woodlands. **CUPLEAF CEANOTHUS**, *C. greggii*

**1b.** Leaves alternate.

    **4a.** Plants with spine-tipped twigs.

        **5a.** Leaves with three veins from base, sometimes laterals less significant; leaves dull green with whitish film above and below or grayish without film below.

            **6a.** Leaves with whitish film on both surfaces, lateral veins sometimes obscure; dry chaparral slopes below 1800 m. . . . . . . . . . . . . . . . . . . . . . . . . . **CHAPARRAL WHITETHORN**, *C. leucodermis*

            **6b.** Leaves with whitish film above, gray below; dry, open conifer slopes above 1500 m. . **MOUNTAIN WHITETHORN**, *C. cordulatus*

        **5b.** Leaves with one main vein, hairless and shiny on both surfaces; dry coastal sage scrub and chaparral slopes below 900 m. . . . . . . . . . . . . . . . . . . . . . . . . . . . . . . . . . . . . . **GREENBARK CEANOTHUS**, *C. spinosus*

    **4b.** Plants without spine-tipped twigs.

        **7a.** Leaves mostly 3-veined from base, more or less hairy.

            **8a.** Leaves serrated, young branchlets reddish brown to olive and hairy or warty on a more villous petiole; western Riverside County and northward; dry slopes below 1400 m. . . . . . . . . . . . . . . . . . . . . . . . . . . . . . . . . . . . . . **HAIRY CEANOTHUS**, *C. oliganthus*

            **8b.** Leaves entire or serrated, young branchlets green to yellowish and glabrous (sometimes strigose) or reddish and tomentose, petioles not much more or less pubescent than leaves.

                **9a.** Leaves with dark serrations at margins, young branchlets reddish and hairy; Redlands area to Santa Ana Mountains and south, in chamise and mixed chaparral below 1100 m. . . . . . . . . . . . . . . . **WOOLLYLEAF CEANOTHUS**, *C. tomentosus*

                **9b.** Leaf margins usually entire to somewhat fine-toothed near tip, greenish branchlets usually glabrous or somewhat pubescent; woodlands on dry slopes and ridges between 300 and 1800 m. . . . . . . . . . . . . . . . **DEER BRUSH**, *C. integerrimus*

        **7b.** Leaves mostly 1-veined.

            **10a.** Leaves usually more than 2 cm long, more than 10 mm wide; woodlands on dry slopes and ridges between 300 and 1800 m. . . . . . . . . . . . . . . . . . . . . . . . . . . . . . . . . . . **DEER BRUSH**, *C. integerrimus*

            **10b.** Leaves usually less than 2 cm long, less than 15 mm wide.

                **11a.** Leaves dull green, smooth above with grayish white fine hairs below; near coast, below 600 m in chaparral. . . . . . . . . . . . . . . . . . . . . . . . . . . . **BIGPOD CEANOTHUS**, *C. megacarpus*

                **11b.** Leaves dark green, smooth above, very fine hairs below; coastal hills in coastal sage scrub and chamise chaparral. . . . . . . . . . . . . . . . . . **WARTYSTEM CEANOTHUS**, *C. verrucosus*

# *Ceanothus cordulatus* Kellogg
## MOUNTAIN WHITETHORN (SNOW BRUSH)

**BUCKBRUSH FAMILY** (Rhamnaceae)

**DESCRIPTION** Much branched, spiny shrub, 1 to 2 m tall, smooth whitish or grayish bark. **Leaves** alternate, more or less clustered bundles, evergreen, ovate or elliptic, tapering to a point at apex, rounded at base, mostly entire, 1 to 3 cm long, 0.5 to 2 cm wide, 3-veined, dull green, pubescent, filmy coating above, lighter green to grayish below. **Flowers** May to July, 2 to 6 cm long, dense white clusters. **Fruit**, capsule with slight crests (horns) 4 to 6 mm across, somewhat sticky before maturity.

**DISTRIBUTION** Dry open slopes, flats; 1500 to 2900 m (5000–9500 ft); in mixed conifer, yellow pine, mostly above yellow pine; San Jacinto Mountains, north to Sierra Nevada.

**FIRE RESPONSE** Stump-sprouts after fire; seed-sprouter.

**WILDLIFE VALUE** Provides staple or preferred browse for deer and bighorn sheep; fruit eaten by birds, small mammals. Poor for livestock, except sheep and goats.

**CULTURAL VALUE** None known.

# *Ceanothus crassifolius* Torr.
## HOARY LEAF CEANOTHUS

**BUCKBRUSH FAMILY** (Rhamnaceae)

**DESCRIPTION** Much-branched shrub, 2 to 3.5 m tall; grayish, brown, or white branches with wart-like protrusions at nodes. **Leaves**, evergreen, opposite, thick, leathery, rounded to spatulate, elliptic, or ovate 1.5 to 3.5 cm long, 0.8 to 2.5 cm wide, commonly revolute (edges curled under), olive green above, white-fuzzy below, coarsely dentate or sometimes entire leaf petiole less than 5 mm long. **Flowers** January to April, white clusters, inflorescences 1.5 to 3 cm long. **Fruit**, roundish, sticky capsule, 6 to 8 mm diameter. Var. *planus* Abrams with flat leaves occurs in Kern, Santa Barbara and Ventura counties.

**DISTRIBUTION** Common below 1100 m (3500 ft); chaparral.

**FIRE RESPONSE** Rarely stump-sprouts from exposed roots, otherwise non-sprouter after fire, obligate seeder.

**WILDLIFE VALUE** Provides staple browse for deer; fruit preferred by birds, small mammals, insects.

**CULTURAL VALUE** Unknown.

# *Ceanothus cuneatus* (Dougl. ex Hook.) Nutt.
## BUCKBRUSH

**BUCKBRUSH FAMILY** (Rhamnaceae)

**DESCRIPTION** Rigid shrub 1 to 3.5 m tall, bark soon becomes grayish. **Leaves**, evergreen on spur-like divergent, rigid branchlets, sometimes several at a node, opposite, sometimes notched at apex or almost entire and spatulate to ovate, gray green, hairless or pubescent above, firm, 0.5 to 1.5 cm long, 3 to 10 mm wide, flat or sometimes rolled downward at margins. **Flowers** white, March to May. **Fruit**, capsule 5 to 6 mm with short erect horns. Primary seedling leaves serrated and spatulate, larger (2+ cm long, 1+ cm wide), less stiff than on mature plants, cotyledons entire and nearly oval.

**DISTRIBUTION** Common on dry slopes and fans below 1800 m (6000 ft); chaparral, pinyon-juniper, Jeffrey pine and ponderosa pine communities.

**FIRE RESPONSE** Obligate seeder, seedlings usually prolific after fire. Can regenerate from exposed roots.

**WILDLIFE VALUE** Important browse and cover. Seeds preferred by small animals, insects, birds.

**CULTURAL VALUE** Unknown.

# *Ceanothus cuneatus* (Dougl. ex Hook.) Nutt.
## BUCKBRUSH

# *Ceanothus greggii* var. *perplexans* (Trel.) Jeps.
## CUPLEAF CEANOTHUS

**BUCKBRUSH FAMILY** (Rhamnaceae)

**SYNONYM** *Ceanothus perplexans* Trel.

**DESCRIPTION** Plant erect, rigidly and intricately branched, 1 to 2 m tall, young branchlets with greenish bark soon become gray. **Leaves**, evergreen, opposite, roundish to broadly elliptical or ovate, commonly cupped upward, 1 to 3 cm long, 8 to 20 mm wide, petiole 1 to 4 mm long, mostly conspicuously toothed, yellowish green, hairless to pubescent or rarely tomentose above, usually tomentose below. **Flowers** March to May, cream-colored clusters. **Fruit**, rounded capsule 4 to 5 mm across, small horns on sides of capsule.

**DISTRIBUTION** Dry slopes below 2100 m (7000 ft); in chaparral, sagebrush, pinyon-juniper, Jeffrey or ponderosa pine, south face of San Bernardino Mountains to Lower California.

**FIRE RESPONSE** Non-sprouter after fire, cutting; obligate seeder.

**WILDLIFE VALUE** Staple browse for wildlife and livestock, especially goats, in winter and early spring. Seeds preferred by small mammals, birds, insects.

**CULTURAL VALUE** None known.

# *Ceanothus greggii* var. *perplexans* (Trel.) Jeps.
## CUPLEAF CEANOTHUS

**ADDITIONAL SPECIES** *Ceanothus pauciflorus* Moc. & Sessé ex DC. (not illustrated) grayish green on both leaf surfaces, margins entire or dentate, cupped, 7 to 15 mm long, occurs on San Jacinto Ranger District and in Lake Hughes, Sawmill Mountain area of eastern Los Padres National Forest (Los Angeles County).

# *Ceanothus integerrimus* Hook. & Arn.
## DEERBRUSH

**BUCKBRUSH FAMILY** (Rhamnaceae)

**DESCRIPTION** Loosely branched, 1 to 4 m tall, glabrous (sometimes strigose) green or yellowish branches, some young twigs, green turning reddish, somewhat pubescent, twigs flexible, not spinose; semideciduous to deciduous. **Leaves** flexible, alternate, either pinnate (1-veined) or 3-veined from base, broadly ovate to elliptic, rounded at base, tapering or somewhat rounded at apex, 2.5 to 7 cm long, 1 to 4 cm wide, olive to light green, puberulent to almost bald above, slightly paler and commonly with some hairs on veins below, edges entire to somewhat toothed near the tip, on petioles 6 to 12 mm long. **Flowers** May to July, white to dark blue, rarely pink, on branched flower clusters 4 to 15 cm long. **Fruit**, somewhat rounded capsule 4 to 5 mm wide, usually with small horns.

**ADDITIONAL SPECIES** *Ceanothus integerrimus* var. *macrothyrsus* (Torr.) G.T. Benson also in southern California chaparral and distinctly 3-veined from base.

**DISTRIBUTION** Dry slopes and ridges, 300 to 1800 m (1000–6000 ft); ponderosa and Jeffrey pine, mixed conifer.

**FIRE RESPONSE** Stump-sprouts after fire, cutting.

**WILDLIFE VALUE** Preferred browse of deer and bighorn sheep. Important forage plant for livestock; valuable honey plant.

**CULTURAL VALUE** None known.

# *Ceanothus leucodermis* Greene
## CHAPARRAL WHITETHORN

**BUCKBRUSH FAMILY** (Rhamnaceae)

**DESCRIPTION** Evergreen shrub, 2 to 4 m tall, rigid spine-tipped branchlets, gray or whitish, bark on young twigs green becoming olive green. **Leaves** alternate, with three somewhat obscure veins, midvein more prominent, 0.5 to 2.5 cm long, 5 to 12 mm wide, petioles 2 to 3 mm long, oval to lanceolate, rounded or tapering to a point at apex, rounded at base, minutely serrate or entire edges, usually hairless, darker above, filmy-white on both surfaces, sometimes hairs on veins below. **Flowers** February to June, white or blue clusters 3 to 8 mm long. **Fruit**, capsule 4.5 to 6 mm wide, sticky, without horns, depression in top center. Seedling leaves serrate, oval to lanceolate; cotyledons entire.

**DISTRIBUTION** Dry slopes below 1800 m (6000 ft); chaparral; mountains of southern California, north along Coast Ranges.

**FIRE RESPONSE** Stump-sprouts after fire, cutting.

**WILDLIFE VALUE** Preferred browse and cover for deer; also bighorn, if stands are open. Fruit staple for small animals, birds, insects.

**CULTURAL VALUE** None known.

# *Ceanothus leucodermis* Greene
## CHAPARRAL WHITETHORN

# *Ceanothus megacarpus* Nutt.
## BIGPOD CEANOTHUS

**BUCKBRUSH FAMILY** (Rhamnaceae)

**DESCRIPTION** Large shrub, 1 to 4 m tall, grayish brown or reddish branches, young branchlets commonly with fine, stiff hairs, soon becoming gray, older **bark** rough. **Leaves** alternate, spatulate to obovate with smooth margins, sometimes notched at tip, wedge-shaped at base, 0.5 to 2.5 cm long, 6 to 12 mm wide, petiole 2 to 3 mm, 1-veined, thick and leathery, sometimes rolled under at edges, dull green and smooth above, grayish white fine hairs below. **Flowers** January to April, white. **Fruit**, capsule 8 to 12 mm broad.

**DISTRIBUTION** Near coast, below 600 m (2000 ft); chaparral where may form nearly pure stands following fire.

**FIRE RESPONSE** Probably obligate seeder after fire.

**WILDLIFE VALUE** Provides browse and cover for deer. **Flowers** used by insects; seeds used by small mammals, birds, insects.

**CULTURAL VALUE** None known.

# *Ceanothus oliganthus* Nutt.
## HAIRY CEANOTHUS

**BUCKBRUSH FAMILY** (Rhamnaceae)

**DESCRIPTION** Shrub, 1 to 4 m tall, younger branches round, reddish to olive, hairy or warty. **Leaves** alternate, evergreen, 1 to 4 cm long, 5 to 20 mm wide, villous, petioles 3 to 8 mm long, oval or ovate to lanceolate with fine serrate margins, dark green above, paler below, scattered long hairs to hirsute pubescent especially on veins below, often with two long veins curving upward to parallel midveins, **Flowers** February to May, blue or purplish clusters. **Fruit**, capsule 4 mm broad, usually somewhat sticky.

**SIMILAR SPECIES Deerbrush** (*C. integerrimus*) may also key out to this species but differs from hairy ceanothus; deerbrush leaves thin, less hairy, usually without serrations, with greenish yellow bark, and branches not reddish.

**DISTRIBUTION** Dry slopes below 1400 m (4500 ft).

**FIRE RESPONSE** Stump-sprouts after fire, cutting.

**WILDLIFE VALUE** Provides browse and cover for deer. Seeds used by birds, small mammals, insects. Insects (especially bees) use flowers.

**CULTURAL VALUE** None known.

# *Ceanothus spinosus* Nutt.
## GREENBARK CEANOTHUS

**BUCKBRUSH FAMILY** (Rhamnaceae)

**DESCRIPTION** Large shrub, 2 to 6 m tall, usually with smooth olive-green bark, main branches flexible, commonly with short, stiff, spine-tipped branchlets angled away from main stems. **Leaves** evergreen, oval to lanceolate to nearly linear or oblanceolate, alternate, thick and leathery, hairless and shiny on both surfaces, margins commonly entire, occasionally denticulate or sometimes with notch at tip (emarginate), lateral veins curve toward tip, 1.2 to 4 cm long, 5 to 15 mm wide, petiole 1 to 6 mm long. **Flowers** February to May, pale blue or white. **Fruit**, globose, viscid capsule 4 to 5 mm broad, with small horns.

**DISTRIBUTION** Dry slopes below 900 m (3000 ft) coastal sage scrub (soft chaparral) and chaparral.

**FIRE RESPONSE** Stump-sprouts after fire, cutting.

**WILDLIFE VALUE** Provides browse and cover for deer. Flowers and seeds used by birds, insects, seeds by small mammals, insects.

**CULTURAL VALUE** None known.

# *Ceanothus tomentosus* Parry
## WOOLLYLEAF CEANOTHUS

**BUCKBRUSH FAMILY** (Rhamnaceae)

**DESCRIPTION** Evergreen shrub, 1 to 3 m tall, young branchlets, reddish bark with matted hairy surface becoming gray with age. **Leaves** alternate, ovate to elliptic, commonly several at a node, 0.5 to 2.5 cm long, 5 to 15 mm wide, petiole 1 to 5 mm long, dark green with some hairs above, grayish green and pubescent to almost woolly below, 3- or 1-veined from base, dark gland tipped serrations along margins. **Flowers** January to May, pale blue to white, clusters branched, 2 to 5 cm long. **Fruit**, roundish, sticky capsule about 4 mm across, usually with small horns.

**DISTRIBUTION** Below 1100 m (3500 ft), chamise chaparral, mixed chaparral; merging with **hairy ceanothus** (*C. oliganthus*) in Trabuco-Bedford Canyon area.

**FIRE RESPONSE** Stump-sprouts vigorously after fire, cutting.

**WILDLIFE VALUE** Provides browse and cover for deer. Seeds used by small animals, birds, insects. Birds and insects use flowers.

**CULTURAL VALUE** None known.

# *Ceanothus verrucosus* Nutt.
## WARTYSTEM CEANOTHUS

**BUCKBRUSH FAMILY** (Rhamnaceae)

**DESCRIPTION** Erect evergreen shrub, to 4 m tall; twigs with prominent wart-like projections. **Leaves** 0.8 to 2 cm long, 6 to 15 mm wide, petiole less than 4 mm long, alternate, round- to deltoid-obovate, sometimes notched at tip, 1-veined from base, dark green and mostly hairless above, paler below with fine stiff hairs especially on midvein, entire or rarely dentate margins, thick and leathery. **Flowers** January to April, white clusters 1 to 2 cm long. **Fruit**, round-horned capsule 5 mm across.

**DISTRIBUTION** Coastal hills and mesas; chamise to coastal sage scrub (soft chaparral); San Diego County to Baja California.

**FIRE RESPONSE** Unknown.

**WILDLIFE VALUE** Unknown.

**CULTURAL VALUE** None known.

# *Cercis occidentalis* Torr. ex Gray
## WESTERN REDBUD

**PEA FAMILY** (Fabaceae)

**DESCRIPTION** Deciduous, rounded shrub or small tree, to 5 m tall; mature leaves rounded, often wider than long, 4 to 6 cm long, 4 to 8 cm wide, entire margins, immature leaves commonly reddish, becoming green with maturity, more glossy and darker above, heart-shaped (cordate) at base, 5 to 9 main veins in palmate pattern, leaf smooth, somewhat leathery. **Flowers** February to April, mostly before leaf development, reddish purple to pink, 5 to 12 mm long. **Fruit**, flat pod, 4 to 9 cm long.

**DISTRIBUTION** Slopes of Palomar, Laguna, Cuyamaca Mountains 900 to 1400 m (3000–4500 ft), becoming more abundant northward.

**FIRE RESPONSE** Not known.

**WILDLIFE VALUE** Browsed by deer.

**CULTURAL VALUE** Bark from young shoots used for baskets, and as mild astringent to treat diarrhea and dysentery (Sweet 1962).

# *Cercis occidentalis* Torr. ex Gray
## WESTERN REDBUD

# *Cercocarpus betuloides* Nutt.
## WESTERN MOUNTAIN-MAHOGANY

**ROSE FAMILY** (Rosaceae)

**DESCRIPTION** Erect open evergreen shrub or small tree, 2 to 7 m tall, young twigs reddish becoming reddish brown, mature bark smooth gray. **Leaves** simple, alternate, 1 to 4.5 cm long, 1 to 2.5 cm wide, petiole 3 to 10 mm long, leaf obovate or oval to elliptic, sometimes tapering wedge-shape and usually entire below middle, serrate towards apex with short protrusions of veins, more or less pubescent or puberulent on both surfaces, dark green above, paler with evident feather veining below. **Flowers** March to May, clusters of 2 to 5 blooms, with cylindrical floral tube, first hairy, becoming reddish brown with age. **Fruit**, achene with long, silky, twisting tail.

**DISTRIBUTION** Dry slopes and washes below 1800 m (6000 ft); chaparral, canyon live oak, interior live oak woodlands.

**FIRE RESPONSE** Crown-sprouts after fire, cutting, very palatable at this stage for wildlife.

**WILDLIFE VALUE** Usually preferred browse for cattle, sheep, goats, deer, bighorn sheep.

**CULTURAL VALUE** Wood used for fish spears, arrow shafts, digging sticks. Inner bark made purple dye, bark used in tea for treating colds, dried inner bark boiled for lung trouble. Young plant powdered and stirred into water for use as laxative (Sweet 1962).

# *Cercocarpus ledifolius* Nutt.
## CURLLEAF MOUNTAIN-MAHOGANY

**ROSE FAMILY** (Rosaceae)

**DESCRIPTION** Evergreen shrub or small tree, 2 to 9 m tall, bark gray or reddish, furrowed with age. **Leaves** simple, alternate, green above, grayish below, somewhat pubescent and more so below, nearly linear to lanceolate or elliptic, 1 to 3 cm long, 0.3 to 1 cm wide, pointed at apex, thick and leathery, rolled under at edges. **Flowers** April or May, one to three attached directly to stems, 4 to 5 mm wide, cylindrical tube 4 to 6 mm long. **Fruit**, 6 to 10 mm long, hairy tail 4 to 7 cm long.

**DISTRIBUTION** Dry rocky slopes 1200 to 3200 m (4000–10500 ft); if fire absent or rare, can be found at lower elevation; one collection made near Mormon Rocks in San Bernardino County at 975 m (3200 ft); sagebrush, pinyon-juniper, limber pine, western juniper, yellow pine, and subalpine communities.

**FIRE RESPONSE** Non-sprouter, rare in chaparral. Usually not found in areas of frequent fire over large areas.

**WILDLIFE VALUE** Preferred browse of deer, goats.

**CULTURAL VALUE** Apparently same as *C. betuloides*.

# *Cercocarpus ledifolius* Nutt.
## CURLLEAF MOUNTAIN-MAHOGANY

# *Chamaebatia australis* (Brandeg.) Abrams
## SAN DIEGO MOUNTAIN MISERY

**ROSE FAMILY** (Rosaceae)

**DESCRIPTION** Evergreen shrub 0.6 to 2 m tall, smooth stems with light gray to nearly black bark, sometimes covered with whitish film. **Leaves** compound, alternate, aromatic sticky fern-like foliage, pubescent, 3 to 8 cm long, pinnately divided into tiny oval segments or lobes. **Flowers** November to May, white, five petals, 4 to 5 cm long. **Fruit**, small rounded leathery achene.

**DISTRIBUTION** Chaparral and sage scrub (soft chaparral) below 600 m (2000 ft).

**FIRE RESPONSE** Root-sprouts after fire, cutting.

**WILDLIFE VALUE** Low value browse.

**CULTURAL VALUE** Native Americans probably used this species like a closely related Sierra Nevada species, **Sierra mountain misery** (*C. foliolosa* Benth.), for treating ailments such as rheumatism, skin eruptions, colds, cough, and occasionally, venereal diseases (Sweet 1962).

# *Chamaebatia australis* (Brandeg.) Abrams
## SAN DIEGO MOUNTAIN MISERY

# *Chrysolepis sempervirens* (Kellogg) Hjelmqvist
## BUSH CHINQUAPIN

**BEECH FAMILY** (Fagaceae)

**DESCRIPTION** Evergreen monoecious shrub less than 2.5 m tall with spreading, round-topped growth form, smooth brown gray bark. **Leaves** simple, alternate, 3 to 7.5 cm long, 1 to 2 cm wide, petiole 5 to 15 mm long, mostly obtuse and oblong or oblong-lanceolate to spatulate, margins entire, yellowish or gray green above, golden or pale below, with rusty fuzz. **Flowers** July through September, ill-smelling male flowers on densely flowered erect catkins, 2.5 to 7 cm long, one to three female flowers at base of male catkin. **Fruit**, matures in two seasons, burr covered with dense coat of long spines, 2 to 3 cm thick, clusters of 2 to 7.

**DISTRIBUTION** Thickets on rocky slopes, ridges 1500 to 3400 m (5000–11,000 ft); in mixed conifer, limber pine, lodge-pole, etc.; San Jacinto and San Bernardino Mountains, north to Oregon.

**FIRE RESPONSE** Readily stump-sprouts after fire, cutting.

**WILDLIFE VALUE** Fruits provide staple food source for birds, rodents. Low value browse for bighorn sheep.

**CULTURAL VALUE** Spiny burrs contain edible nuts.

# *Chrysolepis sempervirens* (Kellogg) Hjelmqvist
## BUSH CHINQUAPIN

# *Clematis ligusticifolia* Nutt. ex Torr. & Gray
## WESTERN CLEMATIS

**BUTTERCUP FAMILY** (Ranunculaceae)

**DESCRIPTION** Woody vine, climbing over shrubs and trees, to 12 m tall. **Leaves** compound, opposite, glabrous, divided into 5 to 7 leaflets, leaflets lance-shaped or ovate to palmate, leaf sometimes not divided or otherwise leaflets may be sub-divided, nearly entire or 3-lobed, 2 to 11 cm long, 2 to 9 cm long. **Flowers** June through August, small, in dense clusters. **Fruit**, numerous, hairy-tailed achene, forming fluffy powderpuff-like ball, very noticeable in fall.

**ADDITIONAL SPECIES** If leaves are divided into threes, it is **pipestem clematis**, *Clematis lasiantha* Nutt.

**DISTRIBUTION** Along streams, moist places, below 2100 m (7000 ft), in many plant communities; coast ranges and Sierra Nevada to mountains of southern California.

**FIRE RESPONSE** Probably non-sprouter or poor sprouter from rootstock, but prolific seeder.

**WILDLIFE VALUE** Low value, mule deer browse.

**CULTURAL VALUE** Infusions used by early settlers for sores and cuts on horses, by Native Americans for sore throat, colds (Munz and Keck 1959).

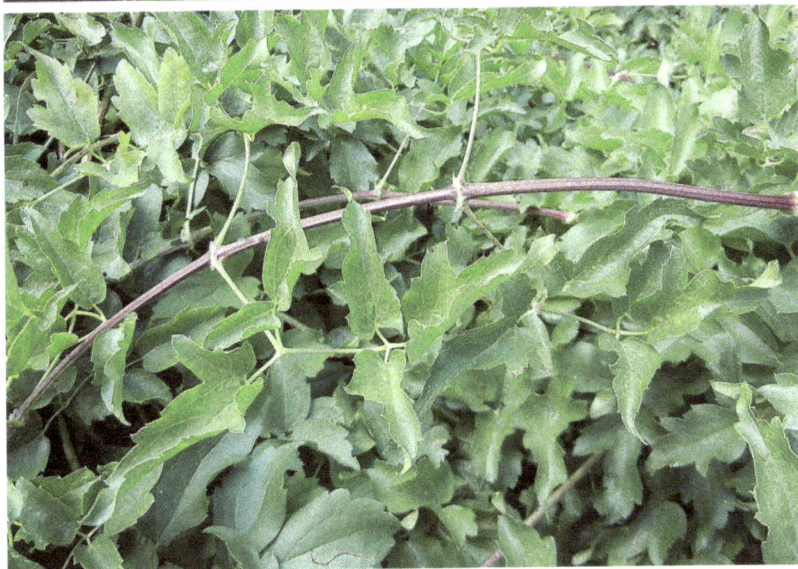

# *Cneoridium dumosum* (Nutt.) Hook. f. ex Baill.
## BUSHRUE

**RUE FAMILY** (Rutaceae)

**DESCRIPTION** Low evergreen shrub, to 2 m tall, densely branched, becoming grayish, branchlets slender. **Leaves** simple, more or less oblong, opposite, may be crowded at tips of branchlets, 1 to 2.5 cm long, 1 to 3 mm wide, somewhat resin-dotted foliage strong scented. **Flowers** November to March, white, four petals. **Fruit**, fleshy, 1- to 2-seeded capsule, 5 to 6 mm long.

**DISTRIBUTION** Below 800 m (2500 ft); frequent on coastal bluffs, on desert slopes of Cuyamaca Mountains; coastal sage scrub (soft chaparral), chamise communities.

**FIRE RESPONSE** Stump-sprouts after fire, cutting.

**WILDLIFE VALUE** Low value browse and fruit.

**CULTURAL VALUE** None known.

## *Cneoridium dumosum* (Nutt.) Hook. f. ex Baill.
### BUSHRUE

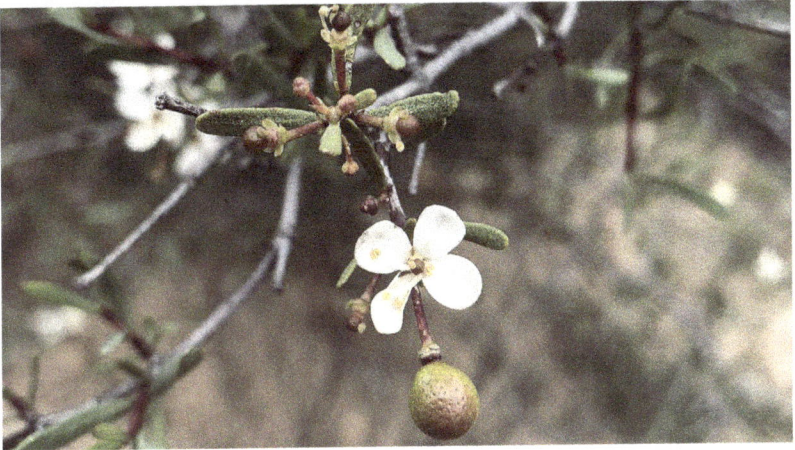

# *Comarostaphylis diversifolia* (Parry) Greene
## SUMMER-HOLLY

**HEATHER FAMILY** (Ericaceae)

**DESCRIPTION** Erect, evergreen shrub, 2 to 5 m tall, young branchlets olive and hairy becoming gray with fibrous and shredded bark. **Leaves** simple, alternate, 3.5 to 9.5 cm long, 1 to 3 cm wide, normally leaf somewhat revolute, petioles 2 to 5 mm long, thick and leathery, oblanceolate to ovate, dark green, glabrous above, whitish-fuzzy beneath with prominent midvein, sharp pointed, finely serrated margins sometimes entire. **Flowers** April to June, white, bell shaped. **Fruit,** warty-skinned red berry containing solid stone.

**DISTRIBUTION** Dry slopes, mostly well below 550 m (1800 ft) along coast; manzanita and chamise chaparral; Santa Barbara County (Nojoqui Park) to Santa Monica Mountains, to San Diego County, Baja California.

**FIRE RESPONSE** Stump-sprouts after fire.

**WILDLIFE VALUE** Low value.

**CULTURAL VALUE** Unknown.

# Comarostaphylis diversifolia (Parry) Greene
## SUMMER-HOLLY

# *Cornus sericea* L.
## AMERICAN DOGWOOD

**DOGWOOD FAMILY** (Cornaceae)

**SYNONYM** *Cornus stolonifera* Michx.

**DESCRIPTION** Spreading shrub, 2 to 5 m tall, brownish or reddish twigs with some short stiff hairs. **Leaves** simple, opposite, lance shaped or elliptic, tapering to a point at tips, 4 to 9 cm long, 1.5 to 5 cm wide, petiole 5 to 10 mm long, nearly glabrous and darker above, covered with short stiff hairs below, obvious lateral veins curving upward. **Flowers** April to November, small white blossoms, clusters. **Fruit**, smooth, white or bluish berry.

**ADDITIONAL SPECIES** If leaves are little longer (10 cm), dark green above and definitely elliptic with considerable soft hairs on underside of leaf and on young twigs, species probably **western dogwood** [*C. sericea* ssp. *occidentalis* (Torr. & A. Gray) Fosberg]. Munz (1974) considered western dogwood more common than American dogwood in southern California.

**DISTRIBUTION** Moist places, below 2700 m (9000 ft); willow and mixed conifer communities; Alaska to Mexico, occasionally in San Gabriel and San Bernardino Mountains (near Pine Knot Station, Big Bear, Lake Arrowhead).

**FIRE RESPONSE** Sprouts readily from underground shoots.

**WILDLIFE VALUE** Low value browse for mule deer, beaver. Not used by livestock. **Fruit** eaten by birds.

**CULTURAL VALUE** Berries probably eaten (Clarke 1977); inner green cambium layers peeled, dried, and smoked in ceremony.

# *Dendromecon rigida* Benth.
## BUSH POPPY (TREE POPPY)

**POPPY FAMILY** (Papaveraceae)

**DESCRIPTION** Rounded evergreen shrub, 1 to 3 m, sometimes 6 m tall, young branchlets with whitish shredding bark becoming dark gray. **Leaves**, somewhat rough, alternate, thick and leathery, lanceolate, 2.5 to 10 cm long, 7 to 25 mm wide, minutely serrate to entire, vertical to axis of stems, somewhat glaucous gray to yellowish green and darker above. **Flowers** April to July, 2 to 5 cm across, yellow, showy with rounded petals, 2 to 3 cm long. **Fruit**, linear pod 5 to 10 cm long

**DISTRIBUTION** Dry chaparral slopes below 1500 m (5000 ft); coast ranges, west base of Sierra Nevada.

**FIRE RESPONSE** Stump-sprouts after fire.

**WILDLIFE VALUE** Staple browse; seeds preferred by small birds, animals.

**CULTURAL VALUE** Fruits, numb gums of teething babies.

# *Diplacus longiflorus* Nutt.
## MONKEYFLOWER

**LOPSEED FAMILY** (Phrymaceae)

**SYNONYM** *Mimulus longiflorus* Nutt.

**DESCRIPTION** Diffusely branched, largely wood subshrub 0.3 to 1.2 m tall. Upper stems and branches, under side of leaves, and pedicels hairy. Yellowish green **leaves**, upper side with impressed veins, leaves lighter below, lanceolate to oblong, may be serrate, 2.5 to 8 cm long, 5 to 20 mm wide. **Flowers** February through August, orange to buff, 5 to 6 cm long. **Fruit**, capsule.

**DISTRIBUTION** Common on dry rocky slopes to 1500 m (5000 ft); coastal sage scrub (soft chaparral); chaparral; inland to San Jacinto Mountains and Kern River area.

**FIRE RESPONSE** Probably poor sprouter or non-sprouter.

**WILDLIFE VALUE** Low to moderate value.

**CULTURAL VALUE** Sweet (1962) reports leaves and young stems of some species used by Native Americans for food and as poultice for sores.

# *Encelia californica* Nutt.
## CALIFORNIA ENCELIA

**SUNFLOWER FAMILY** (Asteraceae)

**DESCRIPTION** Rounded subshrub, more or less drought-deciduous, 0.6 to 1.2 m tall, young stems densely pubescent to tomentose. **Leaves** alternate, yellowish green darker above, ovate to lanceolate, some leaves may have irregular serrations on margins, surfaces with short hairs, tend to be 3-veined at or near base, veins becoming parallel with leaf margins, 2 to 7 cm long, 1.5 to 3.5 cm wide, petiole 5 to 20 mm long. **Flowers** February to July, solitary heads, yellow rays 1.5 to 3 cm long, purple center. **Fruit**, achene.

**DISTRIBUTION** Coastal bluffs, low hills below 600 m (2000 ft); coastal sage scrub (soft chaparral), chamise, etc.

**FIRE RESPONSE** Variable root-sprouters after fire, cutting.

**WILDLIFE VALUE** Low value.

**CULTURAL VALUE** None known.

# *Encelia farinosa* Gray ex Torr.
## BRITTLEBUSH (INCIENSO)

**SUNFLOWER FAMILY** (Asteraceae)

**DESCRIPTION** Roundish subshrub, 0.3 to 1.5 m tall, more or less drought-decidu-ous, brittle stems arising from brown to gray linear-furrowed, woody trunk, branches very leafy at ends, young stems may be tomentose. **Leaves** broadly ovate to lanceolate, rounded or obtuse at apex, tapering to petiole at base, leaf entire or wavy margined, 3-veined from base, silvery-white and felty, 2 to 8 cm long, 1 to 4 cm wide, petiole very short, to 2 cm long. **Flowers** March to May, on yellowish green stalks protruding much beyond leaves, stalks branched, bear several sun-flowers; heads 1 to 1.5 cm across (excluding rays), 4 to 7 mm high, rays showy, 8 to 12 mm long, yellow or orange, 8 to 18 in number falling early. **Fruit**, achene.

**DISTRIBUTION** Inland counterpart of **California encelia** (*E. californica* Nutt.) below about 1200 m (4000 ft), common in deserts and arid parts of western San Bernardino, Riverside, and San Diego coun-ties to Mexico.

**FIRE RESPONSE** Poor root-sprouter. Seeds into available burned over areas.

**WILDLIFE VALUE** Seeds eaten by birds, rodents.

**CULTURAL VALUE** Exudate used as incense in churches in Baja California (McMinn 1939).

# *Ephedra* spp.
## MORMON-TEA

**MORMON-TEA** (*Ephedra californica*), female flowers.

**EPHEDRA FAMILY** (Ephedraceae)

*Key to Ephedra*

1a. Leaf scales in twos; stems bright yellow green; shrub, western edge of deserts in pinyon-juniper and creosote bush between 900 and 2300 m. . . . . . . . . . . . . .
. . . . . . . . . . . . . . . . . . . . . . . . . . . . . . . . . . . . . . . . . **GREEN EPHEDRA**, *E. viridis*

1b. Leaf scales in threes; stems green brown; desert shrub on dry slopes in creosote bush, sage scrub and grassland below 1100 m. . . . . . . . . . . . . . . . . . . . . . . .
. . . . . . . . . . . . . . . . . . . . . . . . . . . . . . . . . . . . . **MORMON-TEA**, *E. californica*

**GREEN EPHEDRA** (*Ephedra viridis*)

# *Ephedra californica* S. Wats.
## MORMON-TEA

**EPHEDRA FAMILY** (Ephedraceae)

**DESCRIPTION** Low, spreading or suberect shrub, 0.3 to 1 m tall, jointed semi-flexible to rigid, straight branches, 3 to 4 mm thick, 3 to 6 cm long between green brown joints, branching at joints into several smaller branchlets 2 to 4 mm thick; leaf scales in threes at joints, mostly less than 6 mm long, about 2 mm wide at base narrowing to point, **leaves** overlapping to encompass stem; most leaves are on vegetative branchlets that arise from branches also with floral and fruiting branchlets, vegetative branchlets smaller (approximately one-half) than main branches, and elongated from overlapping leaves to several centimeters between leaves. **Flowers** February to May, dioecious. **Fruit**, small cone, 6 to 10 mm long, 3 to 6 mm thick, somewhat 4-angled, abruptly pointed at apex, 1 to several at node. McMinn (1939) considered flowering and fruiting bodies to be in catkins; Munz (1974) calls them cones. They certainly appear to be more like small cones.

**DISTRIBUTION** Dry slopes and fans below 1100 m (3600 ft); creosotebush, sage scrub (soft chaparral), grassland; both deserts.

**FIRE RESPONSE** Non-sprouter.

**WILDLIFE VALUE** Used in emergency, not preferred by wildlife.

**CULTURAL VALUE** Tea used by Native Americans and early settlers; tonic for kidney problems, purify blood, and for colds and stomach disorders. Dried stems ground or mixed with pinyon pine resin and used on open sores. Powder made into a poultice for burns (Balls 1972).

# *Ephedra californica* S. Wats.
## MORMON-TEA

# *Ephedra viridis* Coville
## GREEN EPHEDRA

**EPHEDRA FAMILY** (Ephedraceae)

**DESCRIPTION** Erect shrub, 0.5 to 1.5 m tall, numerous broom-like yellow green branchlets 1 to 2 mm thick becoming thicker with gray shreddy bark, several branchlets arising from swollen nodes at 2 to 5 cm intervals. **Leaves** on vegetative branchlets, opposite in twos, tips falling away from brown bases, leaves may be inverted at base, 3 to 10 mm long. **Flowers** March to May, dioecious; **fruiting cones** sometimes 1 or 3, usually 2 at a node, 5 to 8 mm long.

**DISTRIBUTION** Frequent on dry rocky slopes, canyons, 900 to 2300 m (3000–7500 ft); creosote to pinyon-juniper; western edge of both deserts, western slope of Sierra Nevada to Mono and Lassen counties, to Colorado, Utah, Arizona.

**FIRE RESPONSE** Non-sprouter.

**WILDLIFE VALUE** Seasonally important for bighorn sheep. New growth eaten in May, June, July. Used by livestock.

**CULTURAL VALUE** Same as **Mormon-tea** (*E. californica*).

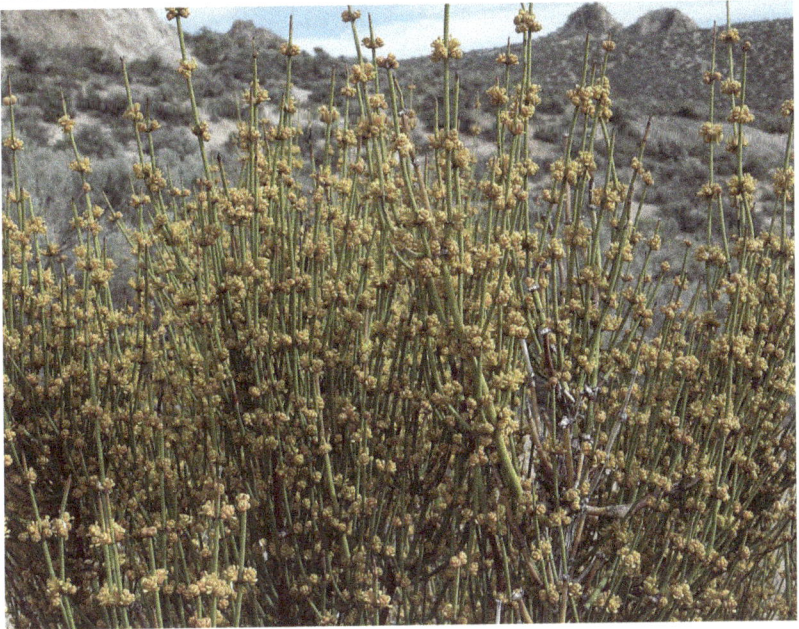

# *Ericameria nauseosa* (Pallas ex Pursh) G.L. Nesom & Baird
## RUBBER RABBITBRUSH

**SUNFLOWER FAMILY** (Asteraceae)

**SYNONYM** *Chrysothamnus nauseosus* ssp. *bernardinus* (Hall) Hall & Clements

**DESCRIPTION** Evergreen mostly wood subshrub 0.5 to 2 m tall, several fibrous-barked main stems from base, gray to whitish, felty branches, leafy, ill-smelling. **Leaves** simple, alternate, with very fine short hair (canescent) especially on young leaves, linear, or divided into linear divisions, 2 to 7 cm long, 0.5 to 4 mm wide. **Flowers** August to September, yellowish tomentose heads, terminal clusters, 10 to 13 mm long, ray-flowers lacking. **Fruit**, achene.

**DISTRIBUTION** Dry benches 1200 to 2900 m (4000–9500 ft); ponderosa and Jeffrey pine, pinyon communities; San Gabriel, San Bernardino, and San Jacinto Mountains.

**FIRE RESPONSE** Variable stump-sprouter after cutting.

**WILDLIFE VALUE** Low value.

**CULTURAL VALUE** Tea from twigs relieved chest pain, toothache.

# *Ericameria nauseosa* (Pallas ex Pursh) G.L. Nesom & Baird
## RUBBER RABBITBRUSH

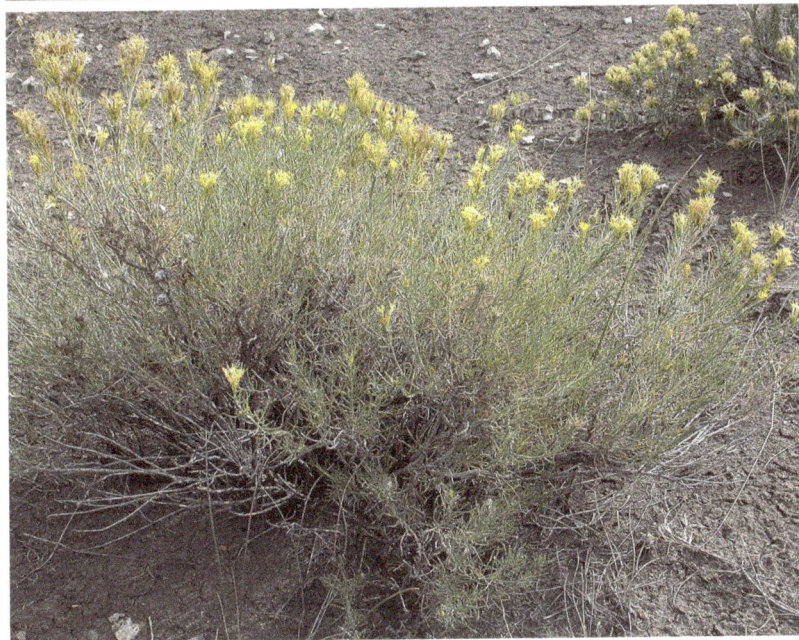

# *Ericameria parishii* (Greene) H.M. Hall
## GOLDENBUSH

**SUNFLOWER FAMILY** (Asteraceae)

**SYNONYM** *Haplopappus parishii* (Greene) Blake

**DESCRIPTION** Erect, branched shrub, 2 to 4 m tall, young stems green turning yellow at inflorescence to brown to gray below, branches hairless, resinous, with numerous glands. Mature **leaves** sessile, usually with shorter leaves in fascicle or bundle, alternate, simple, entire, more glandular than stems, linear to oblanceolate or elliptic, 2 to 6 cm long, 3 to 10 mm wide, flat, thick or leathery. **Flowers** July through October, yellow, all tube flowers in compact clusters of several heads, each head 5+ mm high, subtended by four series of scale-like bracts. **Fruit**, achene.

**DISTRIBUTION** Locally frequent on dry, south-facing slopes or outwash fans and other disturbance areas at 500 to 2100 m (1500–7000 ft); chaparral; San Gabriel, San Bernardino, San Jacinto, Santa Ana Mountains, through San Diego County to Baja California.

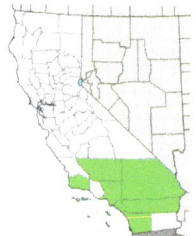

**FIRE RESPONSE** Fire resistant foliage; non-sprouting, may set seed in first or second year following fire.

**WILDLIFE VALUE** Low value.

**CULTURAL VALUE** Unknown.

132

# *Ericameria parishii* (Greene) H.M. Hall
## GOLDENBUSH

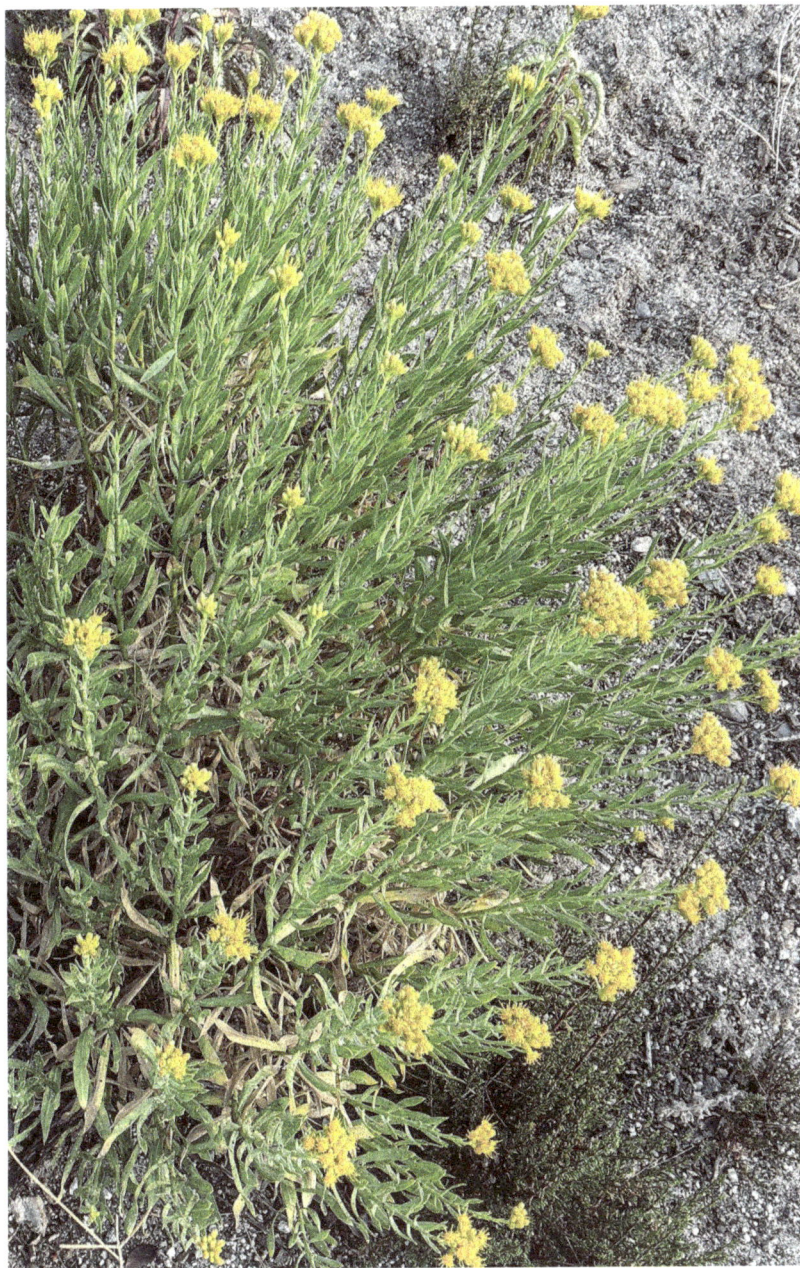

# *Ericameria pinifolia* (Gray) Hall
## PINE GOLDENBUSH

**SUNFLOWER FAMILY** (Asteraceae)

**SYNONYM** *Haplopappus pinifolius* Gray

**DESCRIPTION** Shrub 0.5 to 2.5 m tall, main stem trunk-like; parallel erect branches, young stems yellowish green, resinous, often glandular-punctate, older branches becoming brown. Stems densely leafy, short and long leaves in a fascicle (bundle). **Leaves** glandular pitted, linear to filiform, 1 to 4 cm long, about 1 mm wide, resinous, sticky, lemony smell. **Flowers** May through November, heads in dense or few-headed clusters, 5 to 10 or more yellow rays and many tube flowers. **Fruit**, achene.

**DISTRIBUTION** Washes, dry slopes, 200 to 1600 m (500–5400 ft); sage scrub (soft chaparral), scrub oak, chamise chaparral; San Gabriel, San Bernardino, San Jacinto, and Laguna Mountains.

**FIRE RESPONSE** Seedling response after fire.

**WILDLIFE VALUE** Low value.

**CULTURAL VALUE** Unknown.

## *Ericameria pinifolia* (Gray) Hall
### PINE GOLDENBUSH

# *Eriodictyon crassifolium* Benth.
## THICKLEAF YERBA SANTA

**BORAGE FAMILY** (Boraginaceae)

**DESCRIPTION** Evergreen shrub, 1 to 3 m tall, twigs leafy toward upper ends, young stems grayish green becoming brown. **Leaves** and twigs densely woolly; alternate clusters, leaves of several sizes in many clusters lance-ovate to elliptic, 3 to 10 cm long, 1 to 3.5 cm wide, gray green, darker above, rounded serration on edges, short petioled. **Flowers** April to August, pale lavender, in scorpioid woolly raceme, funnel-shaped, 10 to 15 mm long. **Fruit**, hairy capsule, 2 to 3 mm long.

**ADDITIONAL SPECIES** Var. *nigrescens* Brand appears much like *E. trichocalyx* Heller. **Trask Yerba Santa** (*E. traskiae* Eastw.), common woolly species in Santa Ynez Range and north to San Luis Obispo County.

**DISTRIBUTION** Gravelly, rocky places, below 1800 m (6000 ft); manzanita, ceanothus, pinyon-juniper, communities; Santa Monica, San Gabriel Mountains to western edge of Colorado Desert, San Jacinto, and Santa Rosa Mountains.

**FIRE RESPONSE** Root-sprouts from lateral shoots after fire, cutting.

**WILDLIFE VALUE** Low value.

**CULTURAL VALUE** Leaves boiled into tea for cough, colds, sore throat, tuberculosis, rheumatism; liniment to reduce fever. Poultice of pounded fresh leaves bound to sores on people and animals (Balls 1972).

# *Eriodictyon trichocalyx* Heller
## YERBA SANTA

**BORAGE FAMILY** (Boraginaceae)

**DESCRIPTION** More or less aromatic, evergreen shrub, 0.5 to 2 m tall, very glutinous, resinous branchlets, some young stems may be hairy to woolly, angular, green becoming greenish brown then dark brown. **Leaves** alternate with smaller leaves in leaf axils, lanceolate, tapering to both ends, 5 to 15 cm long, 1 to 3.5 cm wide, hairless, glutinous, darker above, grayish or gray green below prominently veined, margins dentate, sometimes slightly curled under at edges. **Flowers** May to August, dense, pale purple to white clusters, coiled like fiddle neck, 5 to 8 mm long, coils hairy-bristly. **Fruit**, bristly capsule, 2 to 3 mm long.

**DISTRIBUTION** Dry slopes, fans, disturbed places, roadsides, below 2400 m (8000 ft); chaparral, yellow pine, pinyon-juniper, Joshua tree communities; Ventura County through San Gabriel, San Bernardino Mountains, east of Santa Rosa Mountains.

**FIRE RESPONSE** Sprouts from lateral roots after fire, cutting.

**WILDLIFE VALUE** Low value.

**CULTURAL VALUE** Same as **thickleaf Yerba Santa** (*E. crassifolium*).

# *Eriodictyon trichocalyx* Heller
## YERBA SANTA

# *Eriogonum fasciculatum* Benth.
## CALIFORNIA BUCKWHEAT

**BUCKWHEAT FAMILY** (Polygonaceae)

**DESCRIPTION** Low spreading evergreen shrub to I m tall, branches flexible, bark reddish brown, thin and shredding. **Leaves** simple, oblong-linear to lanceolate or oblanceolate, revolute, evergreen, alternate bundles (fascicles), 6 to 20 mm long, 2 to 5 mm wide, margins entire, green above, whitish below, somewhat pubescent above to nearly villous below. **Flowers** May to October, dense white or pinkish clusters, turn red brown with age. **Fruit**, shiny achene about 2 mm long.

**DISTRIBUTION** Common on slopes, mesas; Santa Clara County south to Baja California; in many plant communities; four varieties are recognized in different plant communities from immediate coast to 2100 m (7000 ft).

**FIRE RESPONSE** Seedling response to fire; non-sprouter or rarely from underground shoots.

**WILDLIFE VALUE** Low value browse and seed.

**CULTURAL VALUE** Green young shoots edible. Leaves boiled to make potion for headache and stomach ailments. White flowers steeped for use as eyewash (Sweet 1962).

# *Eriogonum fasciculatum* Benth.
## CALIFORNIA BUCKWHEAT

# *Eriogonum parvifolium* Sm.
## SEACLIFF BUCKWHEAT

**BUCKWHEAT FAMILY** (Polygonaceae)

**DESCRIPTION** Evergreen spreading shrub or branches lying on ground, 10 to 12 cm tall, bark becomes shreddy with age. **Leaves** simple in alternate bundles, somewhat deltoid to orbicular or nearly obovate in outline, 5 to 15 mm long, 3 to 12 mm wide, petiole 2 to 4 mm long, green and hairless above, white and fuzzy below, margins rolled under at edges. **Flowers** May to December, tiny white dense clusters. **Fruit**, achene to 2.5 mm long.

**DISTRIBUTION** Coastal bluffs below 150 m (500 ft); coastal scrub (soft chaparral).

**FIRE RESPONSE** Deep taproot and lateral roots spread to three times area of aboveground parts.

**WILDLIFE VALUE** Low value except flowers for insects (bees); seeds for insects, birds, small animals.

**CULTURAL VALUE** None known, probably same as **California buckwheat** (*E. fasciculatum*).

# *Euonymus occidentalis* Nutt. **var.** *parishii* (Trel.) Jepson
## BURNING BUSH

**STAFF-TREE FAMILY** (Celastraceae)

**DESCRIPTION** Deciduous shrub or tree-like, 2 to 6 cm tall, straggling branches, bark gray or whitish. **Leaves** thin and flexible, opposite, elliptic or ovate, rounded at apex, minutely serrate, darker above, 3 to 12.5 cm long, 2 to 6 cm wide, petiole 5 to 15 mm long. **Flowers** May to July, brownish purple with tiny dots, five petals, 1 to 7 clusters. **Fruit**, capsule 4 to 7 mm across.

**DISTRIBUTION** Infrequent, moist canyon bottoms, 300 to 2000 m (1000–6500 ft); ponderosa and Jeffrey pine communities; San Jacinto Mountains, south to Palomar, Cuyamaca Mountains.

**FIRE RESPONSE** Information not available.

**WILDLIFE VALUE** Not significant.

**CULTURAL VALUE** Unknown.

# *Euonymus occidentalis* Nutt. **var.** *parishii* (Trel.) Jepson
## BURNING BUSH

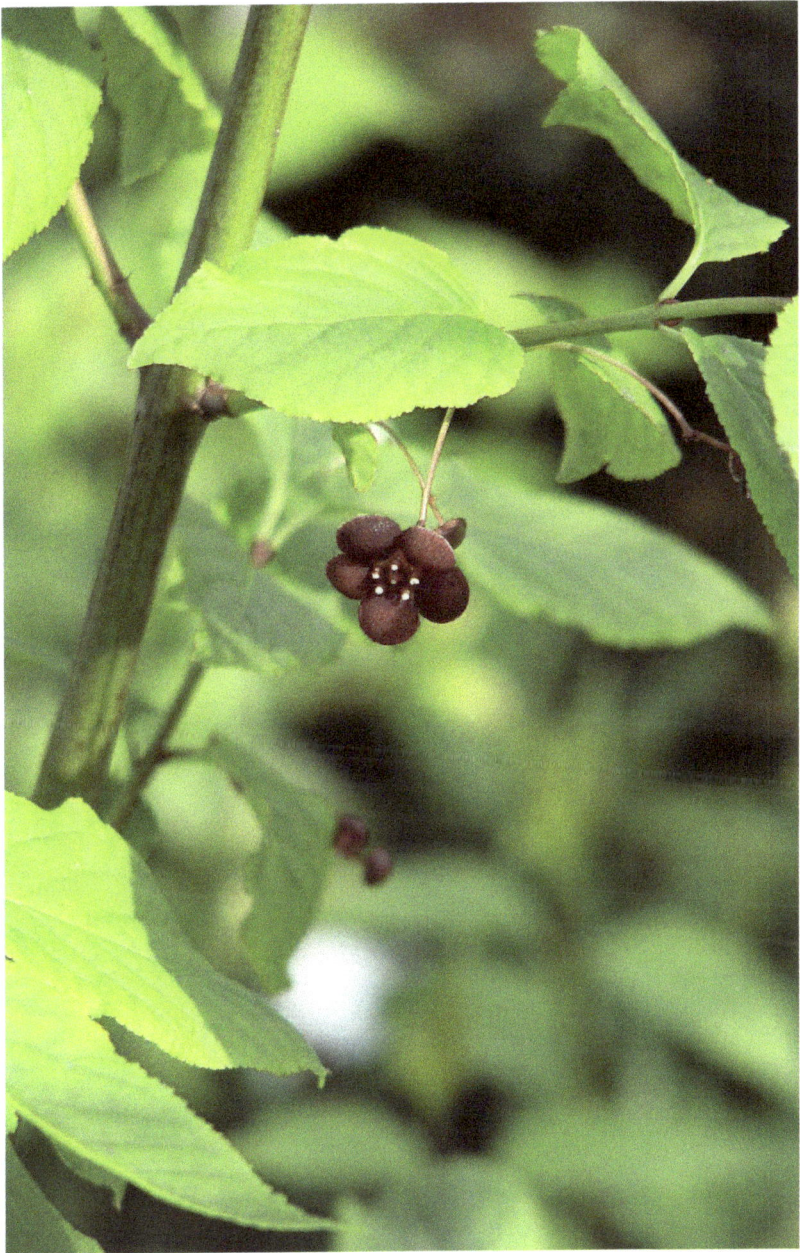

# *Fraxinus dipetala* Hook. & Arn.
## FLOWERING ASH (FOOTHILL ASH)

**OLIVE FAMILY** (Oleaceae)

**DESCRIPTION** Deciduous shrub or small tree, 2 to 7 m tall, erect, 4-angled branch-lets with reddish brown to gray bark, young stems usually pubescent. **Leaves** 4 to 12 cm long, divided into 3 to 9 leaflets, glabrous to somewhat pubescent, darker green above, oblong-ovate, serrate, 2 to 4 cm long, 0.5 to 2.5 cm wide. **Flowers** March and April, numerous blossoms with two white petals, 5 mm long in compound clusters. **Fruit**, samara, 2 to 3 cm long, 7 to 9 mm wide, winged along sides, in crowded clusters.

**DISTRIBUTION** Dry slopes and creek bottoms, below 1100 m (3500 ft); chaparral and riparian communities; Siskiyou County south, Sierra Nevada foothills from Shasta County, south to Los Angeles County, rare in San Diego County.

**FIRE RESPONSE** Mechanism: Stump-sprouts after fire, cutting.

**WILDLIFE VALUE** Staple browse for deer.

**CULTURAL VALUE** None known.

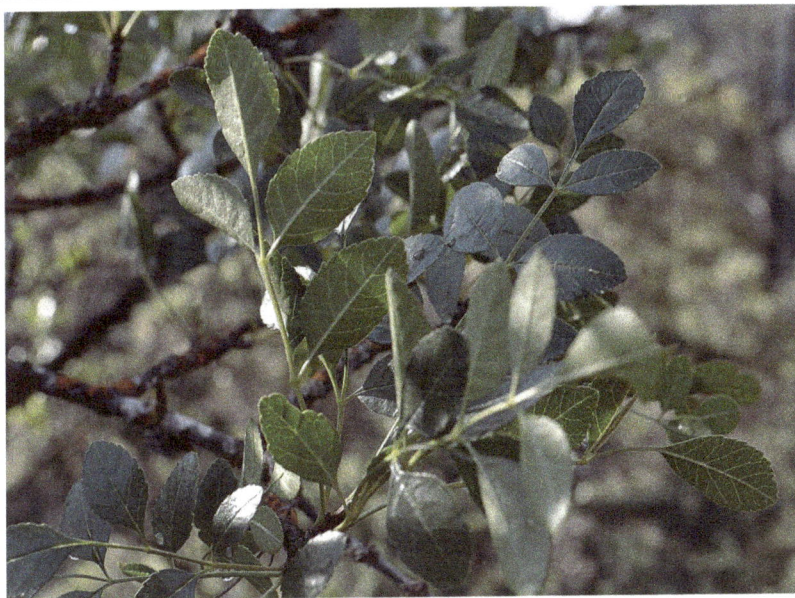

# *Fremontodendron californicum* (Torr.) Coville
## FLANNEL BUSH

**MALLOW FAMILY** (Malvaceae)

**DESCRIPTION** Loosely branched shrub or small tree, 1.5 to 4 m, evergreen but somewhat drought-deciduous. **Leaves** usually palmate or round in outline to elliptic, elliptic-ovate, more or less 3-lobed, dark green above, pubescent above to densely pubescent yellowish below, leaves 1 to 2 cm long, 1 to 2 cm wide, petioles 1 to 5 cm long. **Flowers** April to July, bright yellow, showy, 2.5 to 4 cm broad. **Fruit**, round bristly capsule 2.5 to 3.5 cm long.

**DISTRIBUTION** Granitic slopes, 900 to 1800 m (3000–6000 ft); ceanothus and manzanita to scrub oak chaparral, yellow pine, pinyon-juniper communities.

**FIRE RESPONSE** Stump-sprouts after fire.

**WILDLIFE VALUE** Staple browse for deer, livestock, goats.

**CULTURAL VALUE** Inner bark used as demulcent for poultices to raw membranes (Sweet 1962).

# *Fremontodendron californicum* (Torr.) Coville
## FLANNEL BUSH

# *Garrya veatchii* Kellogg
## SILKTASSEL

**SILKTASSEL FAMILY** (Garryaceae)

**DESCRIPTION** Erect evergreen dioecious shrub, 1 to 2 m tall, usually with white-woolly twigs, young stems greenish becoming dark brown. **Leaves** simple, opposite, leathery, lanceolate to ovate, 2.5 to 6.5 cm long, 1.0 to 3.3 cm wide, petioles 4 to 10 mm long, leaves green and hairless to pubescent above, dense hairs give felty feeling beneath, plane or slightly wavy margined, tending to roll downward. **Flowers** March through May, 2 to 4 dangling strings or "catkins" per cluster, staminate (male) clusters 5 to 10 cm long and pistillate (female) clusters 2.5 to 6 cm long. **Fruit**, ovoid or rounded berry 7 to 8 mm across, buff to reddish brown and pubescent.

**DISTRIBUTION** Dry slopes below 2100 m (7000 ft); manzanita, redshank and other chaparral communities; San Jacinto, San Bernardino (Cajon Pass), and San Gabriel Mountains.

**FIRE RESPONSE** Stump-sprouts after fire, cutting.

**WILDLIFE VALUE** Staple browse plant.

**CULTURAL VALUE** Bark, leaves, and fruit contain the alkaloid garryine, used as tonic whose bitter taste gives rise to some species called quinine bush (McMinn 1939).

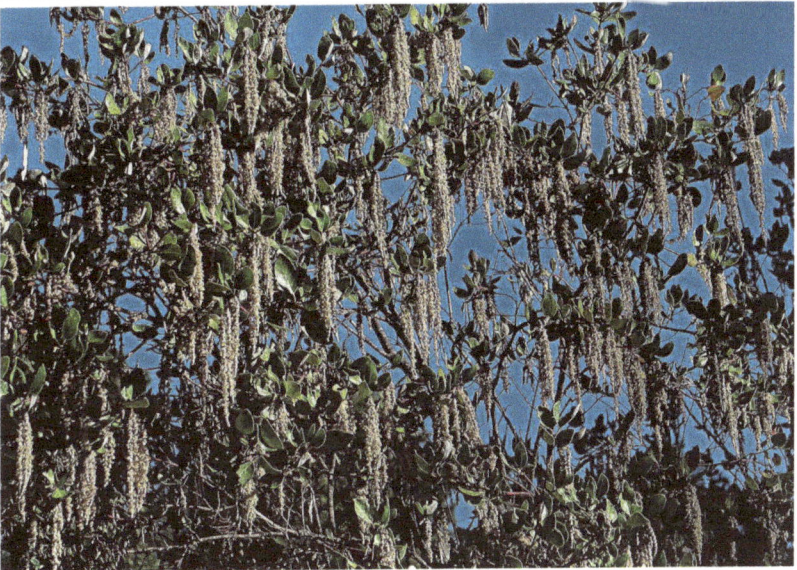

# *Genista monspessulana* (L.) L.A.S. Johnson
## FRENCH BROOM

**PEA FAMILY** (Fabaceae)

**SYNONYM** *Cytisus monspessulanus* L.

**DESCRIPTION** Shrub to 3 m tall, more or less drought-deciduous, angled branches, young branches covered with mat of soft hairs. **Leaves** compound, alternate, tend to be drought-deciduous, 3-parted, crowded on stems, leaflets 0.8 to 2 cm long, 2 to 7 mm wide, petioles very short, leaflets tend to be obovate and nearly bald above and pubescent below. **Flowers** March to June, bright yellow, 1 to 2 cm long, more or less dense racemes. **Fruit**, hairy pod to 2.5 cm long.

**DISTRIBUTION** Exotic from Canary Islands; planted along highways, naturalized near coast, mostly below 150 m (500 ft).

**FIRE RESPONSE** Unknown, probably resprouts.

**WILDLIFE VALUE** Unknown.

**CULTURAL VALUE** Introduced species.

# *Genista monspessulana* (L.) L.A.S. Johnson
## FRENCH BROOM

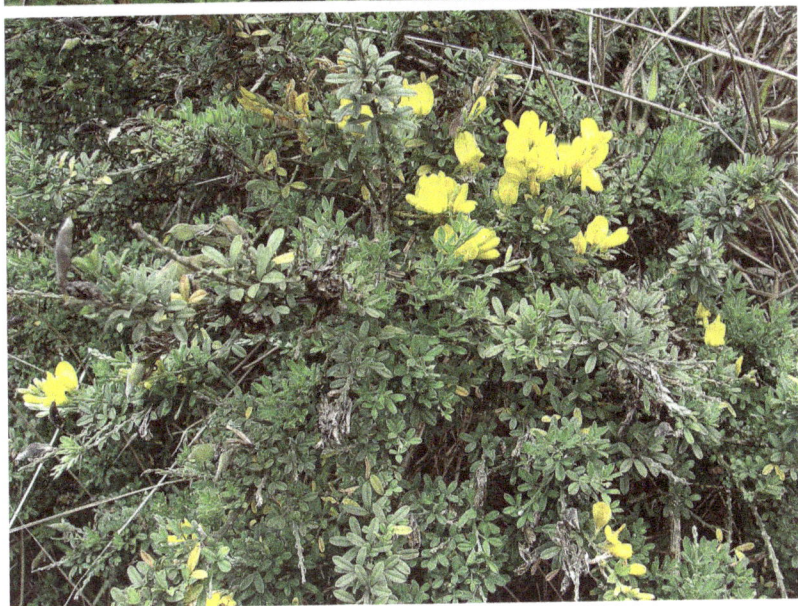

# *Hazardia squarrosa* (Hook. & Arn.) Greene
## SAWTOOTH GOLDENBUSH

**SUNFLOWER FAMILY** (Asteraceae)

**SYNONYM** *Haplopappus squarrosus* Hook. & Arn.

**DESCRIPTION** Low, erect subshrub, to 1 m tall, young stems light brown with persistent leaves, brown with age, bark becomes flaky. **Leaves**, green, somewhat darker above, sharply serrated margins, somewhat rounded at tips, bases clasp slightly roughish pubescent stems, resinous, somewhat glandular, oblanceolate to obovate, 1.5 to 4 cm long, 1 to 2 cm wide. **Flowers** September through October, yellow tube-flower heads with brownish-red hairs in spike-like raceme. **Fruit**, achene. Var. *grindelioides* (DC.) W.D. Clark most common representative in southern California.

**DISTRIBUTION** Common subshrub, open hills below 1400 m (4500 ft); coastal sage scrub (soft chaparral) chamise chaparral.

**FIRE RESPONSE** Non-sprouter.

**WILDLIFE VALUE** Low value.

**CULTURAL VALUE** Unknown.

154

# *Hazardia squarrosa* (Hook. & Arn.) Greene
## SAWTOOTH GOLDENBUSH

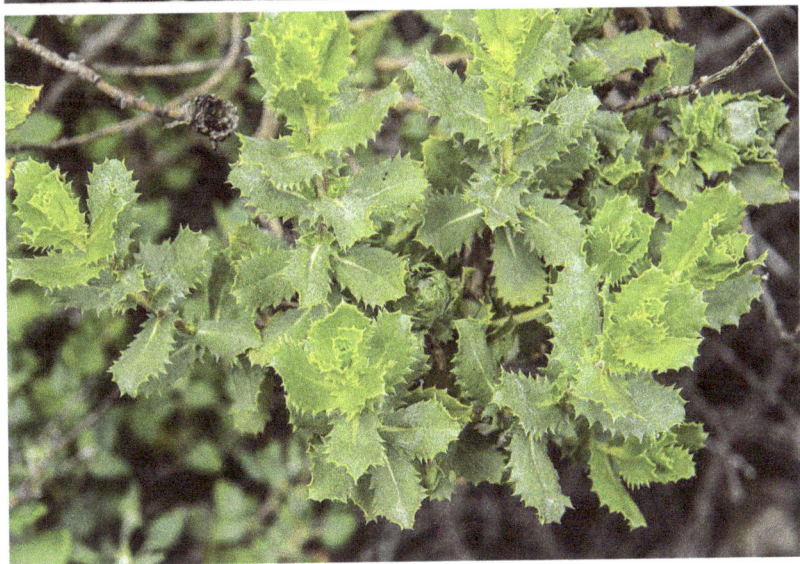

# *Heteromeles arbutifolia* (Lindl.) M. Roemer
## TOYON (CHRISTMASBERRY)

**ROSE FAMILY** (Rosaceae)

**DESCRIPTION** Evergreen shrub or small tree, 2 to 10 m tall, freely branched, reddish to gray bark, young branchlets reddish green to green, sometimes pubescent. **Leaves** elliptic-oblong, 3 to 11 cm long, 2 to 5 cm wide, petiole 1 to 2.5 cm long, leaves may have ligules, tapering at both ends, rather sharply toothed margins, midvein prominent especially below, leathery, flat to somewhat convex, dark green above, lighter below, leaf surfaces sometimes pubescent. **Flowers** May through August, small white blooms, terminal clusters with five petals, 4 mm long. **Fruit**, dry red berry 5 to 6 mm long, most prominent in December, present September through January.

**DISTRIBUTION** Brushy slopes, mostly below 1200 m (4000 ft); chaparral to live oak woodland.

**FIRE RESPONSE** Vigorous crownor stump-sprouter after fire, cutting.

**WILDLIFE VALUE** Low value or staple browse; fruits preferred food of birds, small mammals.

**CULTURAL VALUE** Berries cooked slightly to remove bitterness and eaten. Some Native Americans made a tea to cure aches and pains (Balls 1972). Channel Island fishermen used bark for tanning fish nets (Sweet 1962).

# *Heteromeles arbutifolia* (Lindl.) M. Roemer
## TOYON (CHRISTMASBERRY)

# *Holodiscus discolor* (Pursh.) Maxim.
## CREAMBUSH

**ROSE FAMILY** (Rosaceae)

**DESCRIPTION** Deciduous spreading shrub, 1 to 2 m tall, young stems pubescent and brownish, become ashy gray with shreddy bark. **Leaves** alternate, ovate in outline, dentate with 3 to 7 teeth each side, 4 to 9 cm long (rarely 2 to 3 long), 3 to 4 cm wide, petiole to 1 cm long, pubescent to villous above and villous-tomentose below, green, often with impressed veins on upper surface, lighter green to white-fuzzy, often with prominent veins below. **Flowers** June through August, creamy white, dense branched clusters, 5-petaled, 2 mm long. **Fruit**, achene.

**DISTRIBUTION** Moist woody slopes below 1400 m (4500 ft).

**FIRE RESPONSE** Early successional after fire.

**WILDLIFE VALUE** Low value browse for livestock, deer.

**CULTURAL VALUE** Fruits edible.

# *Holodiscus discolor* (Pursh.) Maxim.
## CREAMBUSH

# *Juglans californica* S. Wats.
## CALIFORNIA BLACK WALNUT

**WALNUT FAMILY** (Juglandaceae)

**DESCRIPTION** Small monoecious, deciduous tree or large shrub, usually with several trunks from or near the ground, 3 to 10 m tall, young stems brownish, pubescent becoming dark brown to gray. **Leaves** alternate, pinnate-compound, 15 to 25 cm long, 9 to 19 elliptic to oblong or lanceolate leaflets, base of each somewhat wedge-shaped or rounded, serrated, 3.0 to 7.5 cm (sometimes 11 cm) long, 1 to 3 cm (sometimes 5.5 cm) wide. **Flowers** March through May, male flowers in catkins 5 to 8 cm long, arise from 1-year-old twigs, female flowers on peduncles arise from end of current year twigs. **Fruit**, walnut enclosed in dark brown husk.

**DISTRIBUTION** Locally common in oak woodlands below 1400 m (4500 ft).

**FIRE RESPONSE** Stump sprouts after fire, cutting.

**WILDLIFE VALUE** Staple browse for mule deer; fruits preferred by squirrels.

**CULTURAL VALUE** Nuts edible. Clarke (1977) indicates Cahuilla Indians used hulls for dye in basket making.

## *Juglans californica* S. Wats.
## CALIFORNIA BLACK WALNUT

Upper, Male flowers; lower, fruit.

# *Juglans californica* S. Wats.
## CALIFORNIA BLACK WALNUT

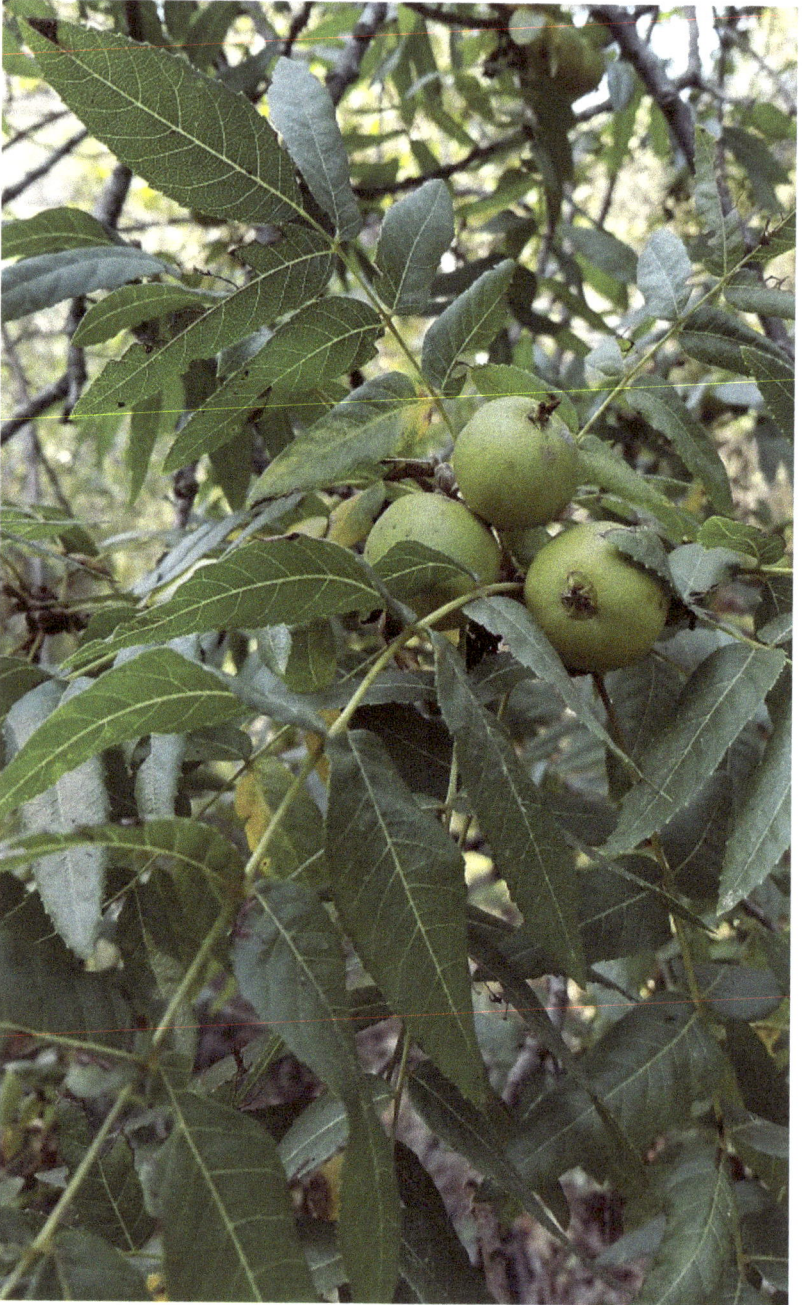

**CALIFORNIA JUNIPER** (*Juniperus californica*)

# *Juniperus* spp.
## JUNIPERS

**UTAH JUNIPER** (*Juniperus osteosperma*)

**CYPRESS FAMILY** (Cupressaceae)

*Key to Juniperus*

**1a.** Leaves with glandular pits on the back; shrub or small tree in pinyon-juniper and Joshua tree communities below 1500 m on desert slopes. . . . . . . . . . . . . . . . .
. . . . . . . . . . . . . . . . . . . . . . . . . . . . . . . . . . . . **CALIFORNIA JUNIPER**, *J. californica*

**1b.** Leaves without glandular pits; shrub or small tree on dry desert mountains and flats, east Mojave Desert between 1500 and 2600 m. . . . . . . . . . . . . . . . . . . . .
. . . . . . . . . . . . . . . . . . . . . . . . . . . . . . . . . . . . . . **UTAH JUNIPER**, *J. osteosperma*

# *Juniperus californica* Carr.
## CALIFORNIA JUNIPER

**CYPRESS FAMILY** (Cupressaceae)

**DESCRIPTION** Shrub or small tree, usually dioecious, much branched, several codominant main branches from base, 1 to 4 m tall, young stems green becoming brown as with **Utah juniper** (*J. osteosperma*), bark ashy grey or reddish, shreddy. **Leaves** scale-like, usually in whorls of three around branchlet, sometimes in twos, opposite, 2 to 4 mm long, bluntly pointed at apex, usually with conspicuous glandular-pitting on back; male cones minute in leaf axils. **Fruit**, berry-like cone, bluish white, turn red brown, oblong-ovoid, 12 to 18 mm long.

**DISTRIBUTION** Dry slopes, flats below 1500 m (5000 ft); pinyon-juniper, Joshua tree communities; desert slopes.

**FIRE RESPONSE** Non-sprouter.

**WILDLIFE VALUE** Low value browse, fruits.

**CULTURAL VALUE** See **Utah juniper** (*J. osteosperma*).

# *Juniperus californica* Carr.
## CALIFORNIA JUNIPER

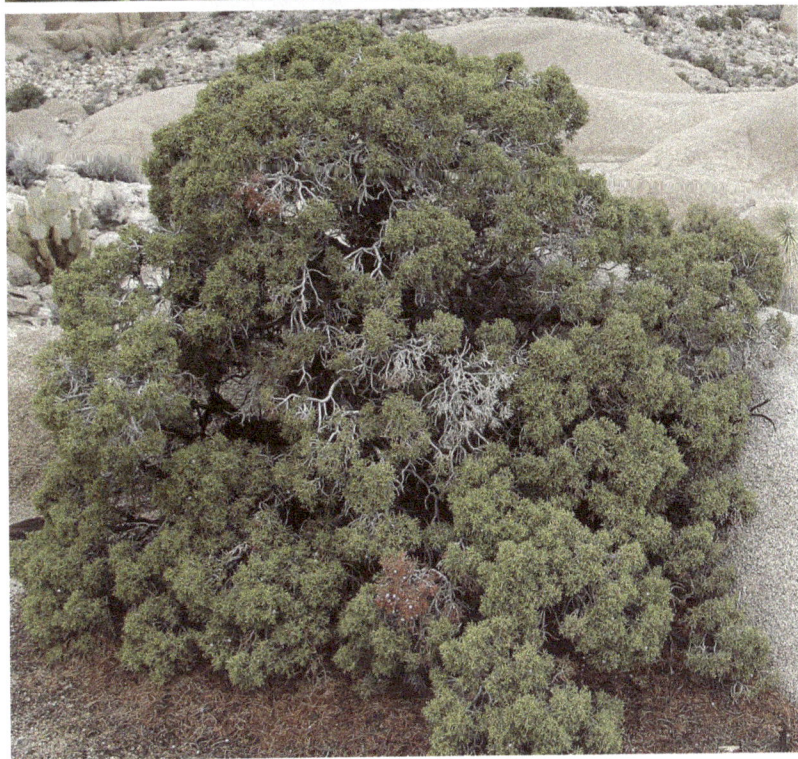

# *Juniperus osteosperma* (Torr.) Little
## UTAH JUNIPER

**CYPRESS FAMILY** (Cupressaceae)

**DESCRIPTION** Large evergreen shrub or small tree, usually dioeceous, 1 to 2 m tall, bushy habit; young stems with leaf scales become brown with age as leaf scales drop; bark grayish, flaky small barbs at branchlet scars. **Leaves** mostly opposite in scale-like pairs, sometimes in whorls of three, 2 to 4 mm long, without glands; male cones, minute in leaf axils. **Fruit**, round berry-like cone, 6 to 9 mm diameter, reddish brown under white film.

**DISTRIBUTION** Dry slopes, flats 1500 to 2600 m (4800–8500 ft); pinyon-juniper; mountains of east Mojave Desert, to Mono County, southwest Idaho. Also on east-facing desert slopes of San Bernardino Mountains.

**FIRE RESPONSE** Non-sprouter.

**WILDLIFE VALUE** Low value browse, fruit.

**CULTURAL VALUE** Berries eaten fresh or sun-dried and ground into flour and made into beverage. Bark used as medicine and red dye made from ashes (Clarke 1977).

# *Juniperus osteosperma* (Torr.) Little
## UTAH JUNIPER

# *Keckiella antirrhinoides* (Benth.) Straw
## BUSH PENSTEMON

**PLANTAIN FAMILY** (Plantaginaceae)

**DESCRIPTION** Evergreen shrub 1 to 2.5 m tall, spreading, much-branched stems. **Leaves** opposite, entire, linear to ovate-elliptic, 0.5 to 2 cm long, 2 to 7 mm wide, firm, crowded, leaf surfaces glabrous to somewhat pubescent. **Flowers** April through June, yellow blooms tinged with brownish red, 16 to 20 mm long, irregularly lobed, snapdragon-like. **Fruit**, capsule containing many seeds.

**DISTRIBUTION** Dry rocky slopes, below 1400 m (4500 ft); coastal sage scrub (soft chaparral).

**FIRE RESPONSE** Information not available.

**WILDLIFE VALUE** Low value.

**CULTURAL VALUE** Bush penstemons (*Keckiella* spp.) probably used like penstemon (*Penstemon* spp.) as wash and poultice for running sores and burns and for floral decorations and ceremonies (Sweet 1962).

## *Keckiella antirrhinoides* (Benth.) Straw
## BUSH PENSTEMON

# *Keckiella cordifolia* (Benth.) Straw
## STRAGGLY PENSTEMON

**PLANTAIN FAMILY** (Plantaginaceae)

**DESCRIPTION** Sprawling shrub, 1 to 3 m tall, commonly with scrambling, long, straggly brown stems, or bushy. **Leaves** opposite, at least some leaves with serrated margins dark green, shiny, glabrous to pubescent, lighter below, ovate or roundish, cordate (heart-shaped base) with prominent veins below, 1.5 to 5 cm long, 1 to 3 cm wide. **Flowers** May through July, red or scarlet, 30 to 40 mm long, tubular, terminal racemes. **Fruit**, many-seeded capsule.

**DISTRIBUTION** Dry slopes, below 1200 m (4000 ft) in live oak woodlands, manzanita and chamise chaparral.

**FIRE RESPONSE** Stump-sprouts.

**WILDLIFE VALUE** Low value.

**CULTURAL VALUE** See **bush penstemon** (*K. antirrhinoides*).

# *Keckiella ternata* (Torr. ex Gray) Straw
## WHORL-LEAF PENSTEMON

**PLANTAIN FAMILY** (Plantaginaceae)

**DESCRIPTION** Straggly evergreen subshrub, 0.5 to 1.5 m tall, rather straight wand-like stems from woody base, white-filmy; bluntly serrated **leaves** in whorls of three, occasionally two, lance-shaped or somewhat linear, often folded upwards along midvein, 2 to 5 cm long, 2 to 11 mm wide. **Flowers** June to September, scarlet blooms, 23 to 30 mm long, tubular. **Fruit**, many-seeded capsule.

**DISTRIBUTION** Dry slopes below 1800 m (6000 ft); ponderosa and Jeffrey pine woodlands, black oak woodlands, manzanita chaparral.

**FIRE RESPONSE** Stump-sprouts after fire.

**WILDLIFE VALUE** Low value browse.

**CULTURAL VALUE** See **bush penstemon** (*K. antirrhinoides*).

172

# *Krascheninnikovia lanata* (Pursh) A. Meeuse & A. Smit
## WINTERFAT

**AMARANTH FAMILY** (Amaranthaceae)

**SYNONYM** *Ceratoides lanata* (Pursh) Howell, *Eurotia lanata* (Pursh) Moq.

**DESCRIPTION** Erect or spreading, usually monoecious shrub, 0.3 to 0.8 m tall, hairy (lanate) on young stems and leaves, white or rusty star-shaped hairs inter-mingled with unbranched straight hairs; young twigs light brown to reddish brown become grayish with age. **Leaves** alternate, sessile, commonly in fasciles (bundled) or often borne singly, linear or oblong, 1.5 to 5 cm long, 2 to 8 mm wide, fascicled leaves shorter, leaves mostly rust colored to most often dull green and more or less darker above. **Flowers** March to August, unisexual, female flow-ers have pair of bracts from which the two styles emerge. **Fruit**, bladder-like sacs enclose seeds, two short horns above, strikingly dense spreading tufts of long silky rust-colored hairs.

**DISTRIBUTION** Flats and rocky mesas above 600 m (2000 ft); creosotebush to pinyon-juniper woodlands, Mojave Desert, eastern slope of inner Coast Range, San Bernardino Moun-tains.

**FIRE RESPONSE** Non-sprouter.

**WILDLIFE VALUE** Staple browse for livestock, burros, etc.

**CULTURAL VALUE** None known.

# *Krascheninnikovia lanata* (Pursh) A. Meeuse & A. Smit
## WINTERFAT

# *Lepechinia calycina* (Benth.) Epling ex Munz
## PITCHER-SAGE

**MINT FAMILY** (Lamiaceae)

**DESCRIPTION** Erect, small subshrub, to 12 cm tall, considerable stem pubescense (sometimes woolly), at least young stems square. **Leaves** simple, opposite, aromatic, more or less prominent veins, 4 to 12 cm long, 2 to 3 cm wide, petioles 5 to 20 mm long, leaves usually lanceolate to obtuse or oblong, glabrous or scattered pubescense above, more or less hairy or pubescent below. **Flowers** April through August, 2.5 to 3 cm long, white to pink with purple spots, somewhat prominent veins. **Fruit**, ellipsoid nutlet about 3.5 mm long.

**DISTRIBUTION** Chaparral and woodlands on exposed slopes, below 900 m (3000 ft).

**ADDITIONAL SPECIES** *Lepechinia fragrans* (Greene) Epling (leaves tomentose) occasional in Santa Monica and San Gabriel Mountains. *Lepechinia ganderi* Epling occurs in San Diego County and looks much like *L. calycina*.

**FIRE RESPONSE** Root-sprouts after fire, cutting.

**WILDLIFE VALUE** Low value.

**CULTURAL VALUE** None known.

# *Lepidospartum squamatum* (Gray) Gray
## SCALEBROOM

**SUNFLOWER FAMILY** (Asteraceae)

**DESCRIPTION** Broom-like shrub, 1 to 2 m tall; except for spring shoots, stems and branches usually hairless, green becoming light brown to gray with age. **Leaves** acute, ovate, alternate scales 1 to 2 mm long, sometimes a small tomentose appendage in leaf axils, spring growth may be quite different, including larger leaves (7 to 15 mm long, 2 to 8 mm wide) with fuzzy to tomentose leaf surfaces. **Flowers** June through December, heads numerous, terminating short lateral branches, bracts of heads papery, overlapping like shingles, flower heads dull white to yellow. **Fruit**, achene.

**DISTRIBUTION** Common in washes, gravelly places, below 1200 m (4000 ft); coastal sage scrub (soft chaparral), chaparral, Joshua tree woodland, deserts.

**FIRE RESPONSE** Unknown.

**WILDLIFE VALUE** Low value.

**CULTURAL VALUE** None known.

# *Lepidospartum squamatum* (Gray) Gray
## SCALEBROOM

**CHAPARRAL HONEYSUCKLE** (*Lonicera interrupta*)

**HONEYSUCKLE FAMILY** (Caprifoliaceae)

*Key to Lonicera*

**1a**. Leaves often joined together in a whorl near branch tips, especially just below flowers or fruits; vine-like shrub, dry slopes between 300 and 1800 m in chaparral, yellow pine. . . . . . . . . . . . . . . . . . **CHAPARRAL HONEYSUCKLE**, *L. interrupta*

**1b**. Leaves all separate to branch tips; vine-like shrub in chaparral below 900 m in Santa Barbara region. . . . . . **SANTA BARBARA HONEYSUCKLE**, *L. subspicata*

# *Lonicera interrupta* Benth.
## CHAPARRAL HONEYSUCKLE

**HONEYSUCKLE FAMILY** (Caprifoliaceae)

**DESCRIPTION** Evergreen bushy vine-like shrub with branches leaning on and growing over other vegetation; branchlets often purplish becoming brown with stringy bark, filmy covered, and hairless. **Leaves** opposite, entire, roundish to elliptic, 1.5 to 7.0 cm long, 1.5 to 5.0 cm wide, green above, white-filmy below, thick and somewhat leathery, uppermost pair often joined at base, forming apparently single leaf through which stem passes. **Flowers** May to July, whorls of terminal clusters, 3 to 16 cm long, yellowish corolla, funnel-shaped, 10 to 14 mm long. **Fruit**, red berry 5 mm diameter.

**DISTRIBUTION** Dry slopes 300 to 1800 m (1000–6000 ft); chaparral to yellow pine forests; north coast ranges to San Bernardino Mountains.

**ADDITIONAL SPECIES California Honeysuckle** (*Lonicera hispidula* Dougl.) with pink purple flowers and glandular-hairy flower stalks also occur with this species.

**FIRE RESPONSE** Probably non-sprouter or poor sprouter.

**WILDLIFE VALUE** Low to moderate value for deer and birds, some use by bees.

**CULTURAL VALUE** Medsger (1966) reported **twinberry** [*L. involucrata* (Richards.) Banks ex Spreng.] berries eaten by Native Americans; no mention made of chaparral honey-suckle or Santa Barbara honeysuckle.

# *Lonicera interrupta* Benth.
## CHAPARRAL HONEYSUCKLE

# *Lonicera subspicata* Hook. & Arn.
## SANTA BARBARA HONEYSUCKLE

**HONEYSUCKLE FAMILY** (Caprifoliaceae)

**DESCRIPTION** Clambering, evergreen, vine-like shrub, 1 to 2.5 m tall, thin shredded brown gray bark on older branches. **Leaves**, 1 to 3.5 cm long, 0.5 to 2.5 cm wide; petiole 3 to 4 mm long, narrowly elliptical or linear to oblanceolate, leathery, darker green and hairless above, lighter below and usually pubescent white, fuzzy below; leaf margins may be rolled downward and somewhat serrate. **Flowers** June to July, pale yellow. **Fruit**, yellowish or red ellipsoid berry, 5 to 7 mm long.

**DISTRIBUTION** In chaparral, mostly below 900 m (3000 ft); Santa Barbara region. Var. *denudata* Rehd. with somewhat broader leaves grows at higher elevation, to 1500 m (5000 ft).

**FIRE RESPONSE** Early postfire successional; non-sprouter.

**WILDLIFE VALUE** Preferred browse for deer, livestock, goats, especially after burns.

**CULTURAL VALUE** See **chaparral honeysuckle** (*L. interrupta*).

# *Lupinus albifrons* Benth. ex Lindl.
## SILVER LUPINE

**PEA FAMILY** (Fabaceae)

**DESCRIPTION** Rounded shrub, to 1.5 m tall, yellowish green pubescent stems becoming brownish to gray with flaky bark and silky-silver foliage. **Leaves** compound, alternate, olive green divided into 7 to 10 palmate leaflets, silky on both surfaces, leaflets 1 to 3 cm long, 3 to 10 mm wide, petioles 2 to 4 cm long. **Flowers** March to July, blue or purple, upper petal with light center. **Fruit**, pubescent pod 3 to 5 cm long.

**DISTRIBUTION** Common on dry hillsides, sandy places below 1500 m (5000 ft); in many plant communities; Ventura County north to Humboldt County.

**FIRE RESPONSE** Important early invader following fire, lasts 3 to 4 years, later only as an occasional plant, coastal species useful for dune reclamation; non-sprouter.

**WILDLIFE VALUE** Low value except for insects, especially bees, small animals.

**CULTURAL VALUE** Though seeds of some species contain poisonous alkaloids, Native Americans made medicinal tea from seeds, especially to help urination (Sweet 1962).

# *Lupinus albifrons* Benth. ex Lindl.
## SILVER LUPINE

**ADDITIONAL SPECIES** **Pauma lupine** [*Lupinus longifolius* (S. Wats.) Abrams] has more herbaceous growth with somewhat longer petioles (4 to 7 cm long), leaflets (3 to 6 cm), confined to lower elevations inland from coast to Santa Ana Mountains. **Inyo lupine** (*L. excubitus* var. *johnstonii* C.P. Sm.), pine woodlands, San Gabriel Mountains, 1700 to 2000 m (5500–6600 ft), longer petioles (4 to 10 cm), usually larger leaves (leaflets 2 to 4 cm long); stems woody at base. Along coastal strand in Santa Barbara County, look for **tree lupine** (*L. arboreus* Sims) with yellow flowers. **Dune lupine** (*L. chamissonis* Eschsch.) is another coastal species with silky leaves.

# *Lycium californicum* Nutt. ex Gray
## BOX-THORN

NIGHTSHADE FAMILY (Solanaceae)

**DESCRIPTION** Compact appearing, intricately branched and densely spiny shrub with numerous small twigs ending in spines, 1 to 2 m tall. **Leaves** somewhat drought-deciduous, grayish green above and below, 1 to 3 in a bundle, fleshy and succulent, hairless, spatulate to linear, 3 to 12 mm long, 1 to 3 mm wide. **Flowers** much of year, solitary, white or purplish, somewhat trumpet-shaped, 2 to 4 lobes. **Fruit**, firm, ovoid (2 mm across), reddish 2-seeded berry.

**DISTRIBUTION** Near coast mostly below 110 m (360 ft); coastal sagebrush in coastal sage scrub (soft chaparral).

**FIRE RESPONSE** Unknown.

**WILDLIFE VALUE** Staple fruit for doves, quail, small mammals.

**CULTURAL VALUE** Edible fruits.

# *Malacothamnus fasciculatus* (Nutt. ex Torr. & Gray) Greene
## BUSH MALLOW

**MALLOW FAMILY** (Malvaceae)

**DESCRIPTION** Tall, somewhat drought-deciduous shrub, 1 to 5 m, long slender wand-like branches covered with short, soft yellowish fuzz, young stems cream-colored becoming gray brown. **Leaves** with yellowish fuzz, round-ovate to deltoid in outline, often presenting an upside-down heart shape, barely to deeply 3- to 5-lobed, with rounded serrations, 2 to 5 cm wide, petioles 0.5 to 1 cm long. **Flowers** April through December, pink clustered blooms attached directly to stems or on short branched stalks; petals 12 to 18 mm long.

**DISTRIBUTION** Dry canyon sides, slopes, below 800 m (2500 ft) or up to 1700 m (5500 ft) for variety in coastal sage scrub (soft chaparral).

**FIRE RESPONSE** Early successional; seedling response to fire.

**WILDLIFE VALUE** Low value or staple browse for livestock, deer.

**CULTURAL VALUE** None known.

# *Malacothamnus fasciculatus* (Nutt. ex Torr. & Gray) Greene
## BUSH MALLOW

# *Malosma laurina* (Nutt.) Nutt. ex Abrams
## LAUREL SUMAC

**SUMAC FAMILY** (Anacardiaceae)

**SYNONYM** *Rhus laurina* Nutt.

**DESCRIPTION** Leafy, evergreen shrub, 2 to 5 m tall, reddish-brown bark. **Leaves** oblong-lanceolate to ovate or elliptical, mature leaves 5 to 10 cm long, 2 to 5 cm wide, petiole 1 to 3 cm long, somewhat aromatic, somewhat glaucous, green, lighter below, usually folded upwards along midvein, like sugar bush (*Rhus ovata*), tapering to soft point; veins, leaf margins, petioles, new growth twigs, reddish; produces new growth before flowering in May and June, hence old inflorescences frequently on ends of branches and obvious. **Flowers** numerous, small (1 to 2 mm), white, dense panicle 5 to 15 cm long. **Fruit**, whitish or greenish to reddish glabrous drupe, 2 to 4 mm long, single smooth stone; frost sensitive, stands occasionally severely frosted with resultant large quantities of dead leaves and twigs.

**DISTRIBUTION** Dry slopes below 600 m (2000 ft); coastal sage scrub (soft chaparral), chamise chaparral.

**FIRE RESPONSE** Stump sprouts vigorously after fire, seedlings common after fire but mortality very high.

**WILDLIFE VALUE** Low value browse. Flowers commonly visited by honey bees; seeds important for quail, wren tits, other birds.

**CULTURAL VALUE** Unknown, probably like **lemonadeberry** (*Rhus integrifolia*).

# *Malosma laurina* (Nutt.) Nutt. ex Abrams
## LAUREL SUMAC

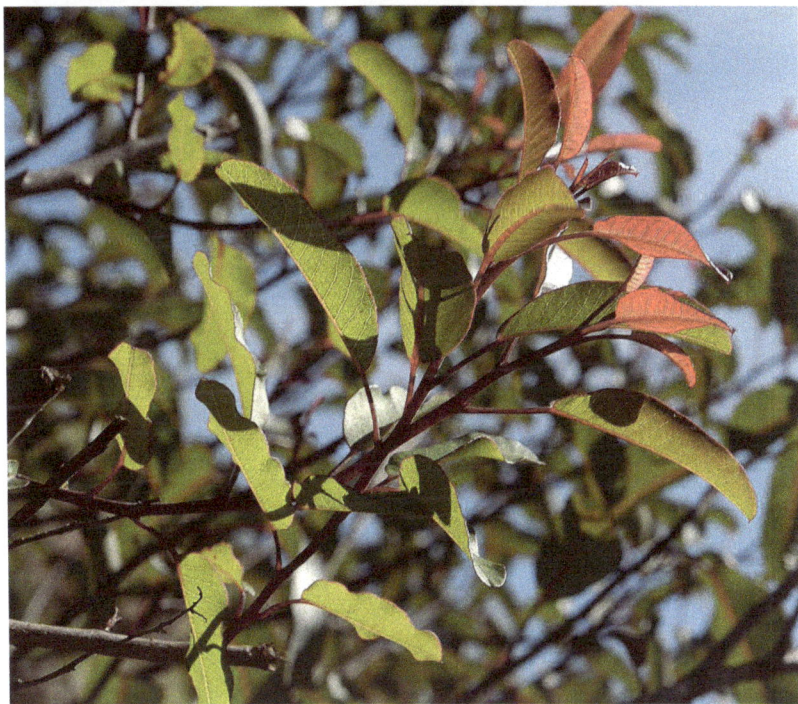

# *Morella californica* (Cham.) Wilbur
## PACIFIC WAX-MYRTLE

**WAX-MYRTLE FAMILY** (Myricaceae)

**SYNONYM** *Myrica californica* Cham.

**DESCRIPTION** Large monoecious, evergreen shrub, 2 to 4 m tall, smooth gray or light brown bark. **Leaves** simple, alternate, elliptic to approximately oblanceolate, glossy and dark green above, paler below, hairless, 5 to 11 cm long, 1.2 to 2 cm wide, petiole short or missing, slightly serrate or with smooth margins. **Flowers** March to May, male catkins in leaf axils below female catkins. **Fruit**, round brownish-purple nut covered with whitish wax, 3 to 8 mm diameter, borne at base of leaves.

**DISTRIBUTION** Moist places; coastal sage scrub (soft chaparral); chaparral, woodlands, below 150 m (500 ft); Santa Monica Mountains, north along coast to Washington.

**FIRE RESPONSE** Sprouts from root shoots, suckers after fire, cutting.

**WILDLIFE VALUE** Low value browse; fruits used by California quail.

**CULTURAL VALUE** None known.

194

195

# *Nicotiana glauca* Graham
## TREE TOBACCO

**NIGHTSHADE FAMILY** (Solanaceae)

**DESCRIPTION** More or less drought-deciduous, tall, loosely branched shrub or small tree, 2 to 8 m tall, white filmy glaucous, green stems and glaucous leaves, easily brush green at touch. **Leaves** ovate or elliptic to almost lanceolate, entire, 3 to 17 cm long, 1.5 to 3.5 cm wide, petiole 3 to 5 cm long. **Flowers** much of year, especially April through September, 3 to 4 cm long, yellow and tubular. **Fruit**, 4-valved ovoid capsule, 10 to 12 mm long.

**DISTRIBUTION** Common, naturalized from South America in waste places, below 900 m (3000 ft).

**FIRE RESPONSE** Non-sprouter.

**WILDLIFE VALUE** Toxic to livestock, rarely browsed.

**CULTURAL VALUE** According to legend, tobacco was one of first plants created by the god Mukat. Leaves used for smoking. Leaves, stems and seeds used for medicinal purposes (Sweet 1962).

# Nicotiana glauca Graham
## TREE TOBACCO

197

# *Peritoma arborea* (Nutt.) Iltis
## BLADDERPOD

**SPIDER-FLOWER FAMILY** (Cleomaceae)

**SYNONYMS** *Cleome isomeris* Greene, *Isomeris arborea* Nutt.

**DESCRIPTION** Erect, rounded evergreen shrub, 0.5 to 1.5 m tall, young branchlets pubescent, greenish becoming light brown to gray. **Leaves** sometimes pubescent above and below, gray green, 3-parted or simple below flowers; leaflets oblong or lance shaped, 1 to 4.5 cm long, 3 to 10 mm wide, ill-scented when crushed. **Flowers** February through May, yellow blossoms, two lower petals more spreading than two upper. **Fruit**, inflated pod, 2.5 to 5 cm long, 1 to 1.5 cm thick.

**DISTRIBUTION** Desert and coastal bluffs and dunes, subsaline places 1200 m (4000 ft); coastal sage scrub (soft chaparral), creosotebush, etc.; also found in Mojave and Colorado Deserts.

**FIRE RESPONSE** Non-sprouter.

**WILDLIFE VALUE** Low value.

**CULTURAL VALUE** Green pods edible and spicy.

# *Pickeringia montana* Nutt. ex Torr. & Gray
## CHAPARRAL-PEA

**PEA FAMILY** (Fabaceae)

**DESCRIPTION** Evergreen shrub, 0.5 to 2 mm tall, densely branched, spine-tipped branchlets, greenish or grayish becoming reddish to gray. **Leaves** alternate, compound, 3-parted or some solitary, green, mostly glabrous or pubescent, leaflets entire, obovate, firm 4 to 12 mm long, 3 to 5 m wide, attached directly to stems. **Flowers** May to June, rose to purple, five irregular petals with yellowish spot near base of upper petal. **Fruit**, pod 3 to 5 cm long, constricted between seeds. San Bernardino and eastern San Diego counties variant have pubescent to canescent leaves and young twigs (Munz 1974).

**DISTRIBUTION** Dry slopes, ridges below 1500 m (5000 ft); manzanita to live woodlands; Sierra Nevadas, Butte County, south to San Diego County.

**FIRE RESPONSE** Sprouts from exposed roots, root shoots.

**WILDLIFE VALUE** Low value.

**CULTURAL VALUE** None known.

# *Pickeringia montana* Nutt. ex Torr. & Gray
## CHAPARRAL-PEA

DESERT ALMOND (*Prunus fasciculata*)

**ROSE FAMILY** (Rosaceae)

*Key to Prunus*

**1a**. Plants evergreen; leathery, holly-like leaves; shrub or small tree on dry foothills in chaparral to live oak woodlands below 1500 m.....................
...................................**HOLLYLEAF CHERRY**, *P. ilicifolia*

**1b**. Plants deciduous; not with leathery leaves.

  **2a**. Shrubby, with spine-tipped branchlets; shrub on desert slopes in creosote bush, Joshua tree, pinyon-juniper between 970 and 1800 m.........
..................................**DESERT ALMOND**, *P. fasciculata*

  **2b**. Shrubby or small trees, not spiny.

    **3a**. Leaves 1 to 2.5 cm wide; petioles short, 5 mm long; shrub or tree on moist chaparral to pine woodland slopes below 2700 m. ...........
.................................**BITTER CHERRY**, *P. emarginata*

    **3b**. Leaves 2 to 5 cm wide; petioles 1 to 2 cm long; shrub or tree on moist slopes in chaparral to oak and pine woodlands below 2500 m. .
.............**WESTERN CHOKE CHERRY** *P. virginiana* ssp. *demissa*

# *Prunus emarginata* (Dougl.) Eaton
## BITTER CHERRY

**ROSE FAMILY** (Rosaceae)

**DESCRIPTION** Deciduous shrub or tree, 1 to 6 m tall, hairless red twigs, older bark smooth. **Leaves** simple, alternate, grouped or somewhat bundled, spatulate to ovate, rounded at apex, 2 to 5 cm long, 1 to 2 cm wide, petiole less than 1 cm long, light green both sides, smooth surface, possible slightly pubescent especially below, minutely serrate. **Flowers** April and May, 1.5 to 4 cm long, five white petals, 5 to 7 mm long, clusters of 3 to 10. **Fruit**, red bitter drupe 6 to 8 mm diameter, turning black at maturity, stone pointed at ends.

**DISTRIBUTION** Moist slopes, stream banks, below 2700 m (9000 ft); yellow pine woodlands, manzanita and other chaparral communities; southern California, coast ranges, Sierra Nevada, to British Columbia, Nevada, Arizona.

**FIRE RESPONSE** Stump-sprouts after fire, cutting.

**WILDLIFE VALUE** Preferred browse of deer; fruits staple for birds.

**CULTURAL VALUE** Fruits used, but bitter.

# *Prunus emarginata* (Dougl.) Eaton
## BITTER CHERRY

# *Prunus fasciculata* (Torr.) Gray
## DESERT ALMOND

**ROSE FAMILY** (Rosaceae)

**DESCRIPTION** Rigidly much-branched deciduous shrub, 1 to 3 m tall, with short, stiff, thorn-like twigs, brownish branchlets becoming gray. **Leaves** simple, alternate, bundles of 3 to 7 or more, spatulate to oblance-spatulate, usually widest near end, 5 to 15 mm long, 2 to 4 mm wide, pale green above and below, slightly pubescent to glabrous. **Flowers** April and May, single or few-flowered clusters, five white petals, 2 to 3 mm long. **Fruit**, dry ovoid drupe 8 to 12 mm long, pubescent with light brown hairs and smooth stone.

**DISTRIBUTION** Desert slopes, mostly 970 to 1800 m (3200–6000 ft); creosote bush, Joshua tree to pinyon-juniper woodlands; Mojave and Colorado Deserts, Arizona, Utah.

**FIRE RESPONSE** Root-sprouts after fire, cutting.

**WILDLIFE VALUE** Low value browse.

**CULTURAL VALUE** Fruits eaten, not preferred.

# *Prunus ilicifolia* (Nutt. ex Hook. & Arn.) D. Dietr.
## HOLLYLEAF CHERRY

**ROSE FAMILY** (Rosaceae)

**DESCRIPTION** Evergreen shrub or small tree, 1 to 8 m tall, twigs gray or reddish brown. **Leaves** simple, alternate, thick, leathery, 2 to 7 cm long, 2 to 4 cm wide, petiole 0.5 to 1.5 cm long, mature leaves generally with coarse spiny-toothed margins, ovate to oval, dark green, shiny above, paler below. **Flowers** April and May, 3 to 10 cm long cylindrical clusters of white 5-petaled blossoms. **Fruit**, purplish drupe 2 to 3 cm across, pulp, thin and sweetish.

**DISTRIBUTION** Dry foothills, below 1500 m (5000 ft); chaparral, scrub oak, live oak woodlands; coast ranges.

**FIRE RESPONSE** Stump-sprouts vigorously after fire.

**WILDLIFE VALUE** Preferred browse of deer and bighorn sheep. Fruits preferred food of birds, animals.

**CULTURAL VALUE** Fruits sweet, eaten raw or peeled, dried, and stored. Pit ground for flour.

# *Prunus ilicifolia* (Nutt. ex Hook. & Arn.) D. Dietr.
## HOLLYLEAF CHERRY

# *Prunus virginiana* L. **var.** *demissa* (Nutt.) Torr.
## WESTERN CHOKE CHERRY

**ROSE FAMILY** (Rosaceae)

**DESCRIPTION** Large shrub or small tree, 1 to 5 m tall, deciduous with smooth gray brown bark, minutely hairy twigs. **Leaves** simple, alternate, light green, lighter below, glabrous above, finely pubescent below, ovate, or broadly elliptic, finely toothed edges, abruptly pointed at apex, rounded or slightly indented at base, 5 to 10 cm long, 1.5 to 2.5 (rarely up to 5) cm wide. **Flowers** May through July, white petals 5 to 6 mm broad, many-flowered clusters 5 to 11 cm long. **Fruit**, dark red cherry 5 to 6 mm thick, bitter, with smooth round stone.

**DISTRIBUTION** Moist, brushy slopes, below 2500 m (8200 ft); yellow pine, live oak, black oak forests or woodlands, ceanothus chaparral.

**FIRE RESPONSE** Shallow-rooted; spreads by rhizomes; sprouts from rhizomes after fire.

**WILDLIFE VALUE** Staple browse, toxic if overgrazed by livestock; fruits preferred by birds, small mammals, black or brown bear.

**CULTURAL VALUE** Fruit can be eaten raw, but slightly astringent.

# *Prunus virginiana* L. **var. *demissa*** (Nutt.) Torr.
## WESTERN CHOKE CHERRY

# *Purshia tridentata* var. *glandulosa* (Curran) M.E. Jones
## BITTERBRUSH

**ROSE FAMILY** (Rosaceae)

**SYNONYM** *Purshia glandulosa* Curran

**DESCRIPTION** Erect evergreen shrub, 1 to 2.5 m tall, gray or brown bark, not very shreddy, young twigs glabrous and glandular; simple **leaves** and short vegetative stems alternate, 0.5 to 1 cm long, 3-cleft, tend to be rolled under at edges, in crowded fascicle-like clusters, somewhat darker green with glandular pits above, slightly fuzzy below. **Flowers** April to June, solitary, terminal blossoms with five pale yellow or white petals, 6 to 8 mm long. **Fruit**, hairy achene.

**DISTRIBUTION** Transmontane dry slopes 900 to 2700 m (2800–9000 ft); chaparral to Joshua tree, pinyon-juniper, or juniper woodlands; western Colorado Desert, Cajon Pass, Mojave Desert to Mono County, Nevada, Arizona.

**FIRE RESPONSE** Variable stump-sprouter.

**WILDLIFE VALUE** Staple browse for livestock, deer.

**CULTURAL VALUE** None known.

# *Purshia tridentata* var. *glandulosa* (Curran) M.E. Jones
## BITTERBRUSH

# *Quercus* spp.
## SHRUB OAKS

**SCRUB OAK** (*Quercus dumosa*)

**BEECH FAMILY** (Fagaceae)

Approx. 20 species (plus a number of hybrids) native to California. Usually tree-like, the two taxa described here are shrubs found in exposed environmental conditions and subject to frequent fire.

**WILDLIFE VALUE** Young shoots and leaves preferred browse of deer, bighorn sheep, cattle, goats. Acorns important food for many birds, small mammals.

**CULTURAL VALUE** Acorns provided staple food for Native Americans. Nuts hulled, ground, leached to remove water soluble tannins, and used as flour for baking or in soups. Bark and some insect galls used for various medicinal purposes, making dye, curing hides (Balls 1972).

*Key to Quercus*

**1a.** Leaves green on both surfaces, slightly paler below, lacking fuzz of any kind; shrub or small tree in chaparral up to 1500 m elevation. . . . . . . . . . . . . . . . . . . . . .
. . . . . . . . . . . . . . . . . . . . . . . . **INTERIOR LIVE OAK**, *Q. wislizenii* var. *frutescens*

**1b.** Leaves dark green above, pale and minutely fuzzy below, 1.2 to 4 cm long; thin-walled acorn cup encloses about half the nut; common shrub or small tree on dry chaparral slopes below 1500 m. . . . . . . . . . . . . . . **SCRUB OAK**, *Q. dumosa*

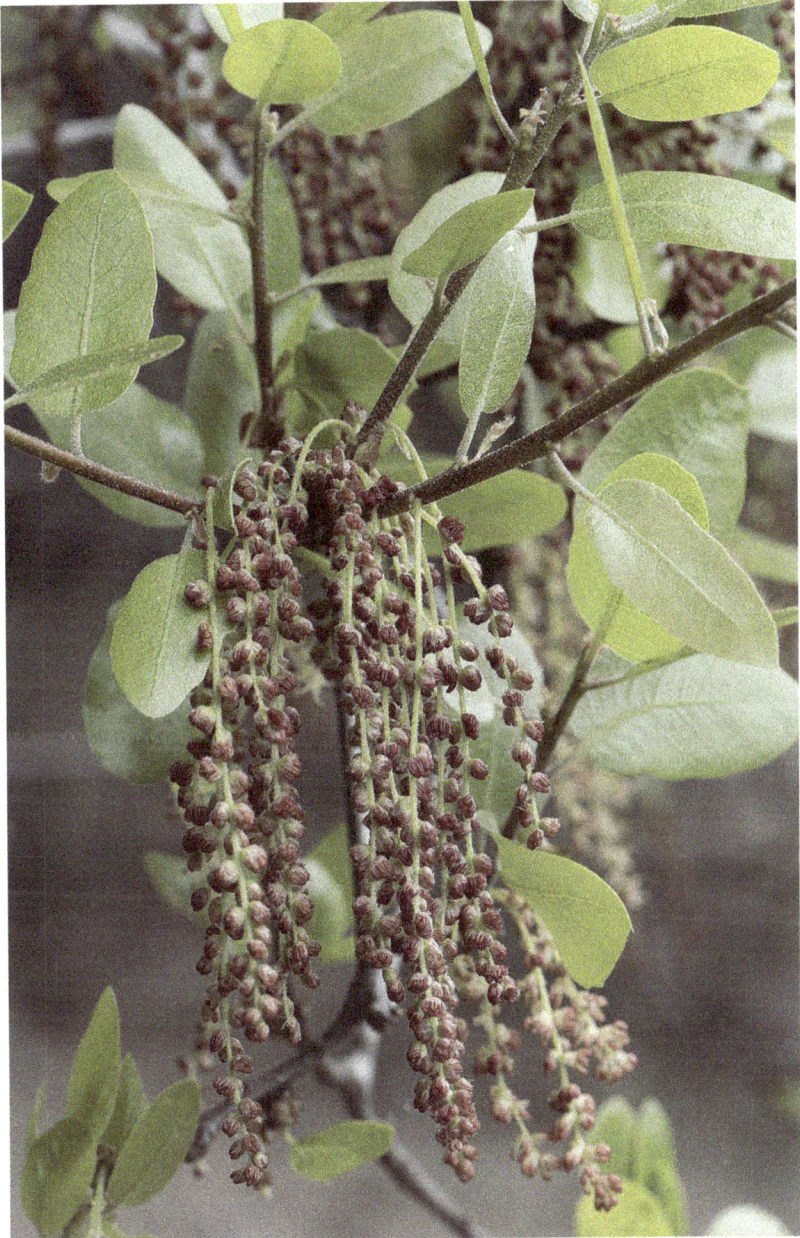

**INTERIOR LIVE OAK** (*Quercus wislizenii* var. *frutescens*), male flowers.

# *Quercus dumosa* Nutt.
## CALIFORNIA SCRUB OAK

**BEECH FAMILY** (Fagaceae)

**DESCRIPTION** Evergreen, monoecious shrub or small tree, 1 to 3 m tall, young stems reddish brown becoming dark brown to grayish brown. **Leaves** simple and alternate, shape and size variable, oblong or roundish to spatulate, 1.2 to 4.0 cm long, 6 to 20 mm broad, petiole 3 to 5 mm long, brittle to leathery and thick, plane or undulate, sometimes dentate, green, shiny, hairless above, may be concave, paler and pubescent below. **Flowers** March to May, male flowers in catkins 2.5 to 5 cm long, female flowers in clusters of 2 to 3 in axils of upper leaves. **Acorn**, ovoid and rounded or acute at apex, matures in one season, with cup enclosing up to one-half of the acorn, cup scales ovate or united at least near base.

**SIMILAR SPECIES** **Palmer oak** [*Q. palmeri* (Engelm.) Engelm.] with wavy-margined, spiny leaves; acorn cup flares out and away from nut around rim; localized in San Jacinto, San Bernardino Mountains at Coxey Meadow.

**DISTRIBUTION** Dry slopes below 1500 m (5000 ft); uncommon.

**FIRE RESPONSE** Stump-sprouts after fire, cutting.

**WILDLIFE VALUE** See genus.

**CULTURAL VALUE** See genus.

# *Quercus wislizenii* A. DC. var. *frutescens* Engelm.
## INTERIOR LIVE OAK

**BEECH FAMILY** (Fagaceae)

**DESCRIPTION** Small evergreen monoecious tree or sometimes shrubby (1 to 5 m tall), young twigs green to reddish becoming gray. **Leaves** usually convex, ovate or oblong to lanceolate, plane or slightly wavy, margin entire to dentate, dark green above, green and somewhat paler and hairless below, 2 to 6 cm long (mostly 3 to 4 cm), 1 to 2.5 cm wide, petiole 2 to 5 mm long. **Flowers** March to May, male flowers in catkins 2 to 5 cm long, female flowers in clusters of 2 to 4 in upper leaf axils. **Acorns** oblong-ovate and abruptly pointed, maturing second season, cup, 8 to 12 mm wide, 12 to 18 mm long.

**DISTRIBUTION** Chaparral, valleys, slopes, below 1500 m (5000 ft); lower slopes of Sierra Nevada.

**FIRE RESPONSE** Stump-sprouts after fire, cutting.

**WILDLIFE VALUE** See genus.

**CULTURAL VALUE** See genus.

218

# Quercus wislizenii A. DC. var. frutescens Engelm.
## INTERIOR LIVE OAK

# *Rhamnus californica* Esch.
## COFFEEBERRY

**BUCKTHORN FAMILY** (Rhamnaceae)

**SYNONYM** *Frangula californica* (Eschsch.) A. Gray

**DESCRIPTION** Shrub, 1 to 4 m tall, persistent leaves, bark on young twigs reddish. **Leaves** alternate, flat to somewhat revolute, oval or elliptic, taper to a point or obtuse, 2.5 to 8 (up to 10) cm long, 1 to 3 cm wide, usually glabrous, dark green above, glabrous or with few hairs, paler below with prominent midvein below, sometimes rusty or pale green, sometimes minutely serrate. **Flowers** April through June, small and greenish, usually without petals, less than 3 mm long, 6to 50-flower clusters. **Fruit**, green, black, or red, juicy berry with two "coffee-bean" seeds, 7 to 9 mm long.

**DISTRIBUTION** Hillsides and ravine riparian areas, 1200 to 2100 m (4000–7000 ft); mixed conifer to redwood forests, chaparral; east and west slopes of Sierras.

**FIRE RESPONSE** Stump-sprouts after fire, cutting.

**WILDLIFE VALUE** Staple browse; fruits, preferred food of birds, bears.

**CULTURAL VALUE** Berries edible and sweet, laxative effect.

# *Rhamnus californica* Esch.
## COFFEEBERRY

# *Rhamnus crocea* Nutt.
## REDBERRY

**BUCKTHORN FAMILY** (Rhamnaceae)

**DESCRIPTION** Densely branched evergreen shrub, to 2 m tall, stiff, relatively divaricate gray branchlets often ending with a sharp point. **Leaves** often in bundles and dark green above (sometimes lighter), yellowish green below, leaves usually feel leathery, ovate or nearly round, 5 to 15 mm long, 3 to 6 mm wide, usually glabrous or slightly pubescent below with smooth margins or often serrated. **Flowers** February to April, greenish, tiny, small clusters from the leaf axils. **Fruit**, red berry, 5 to 6 mm long with two seeds.

**DISTRIBUTION** Dry slopes, below 900 m (3000 ft); coastal sage scrub (soft chaparral).

**FIRE RESPONSE** Stump-sprouts after fire.

**WILDLIFE VALUE** Preferred browse of deer, livestock.

**CULTURAL VALUE** Berries edible, bark was peeled, ground, dried, and used as laxative.

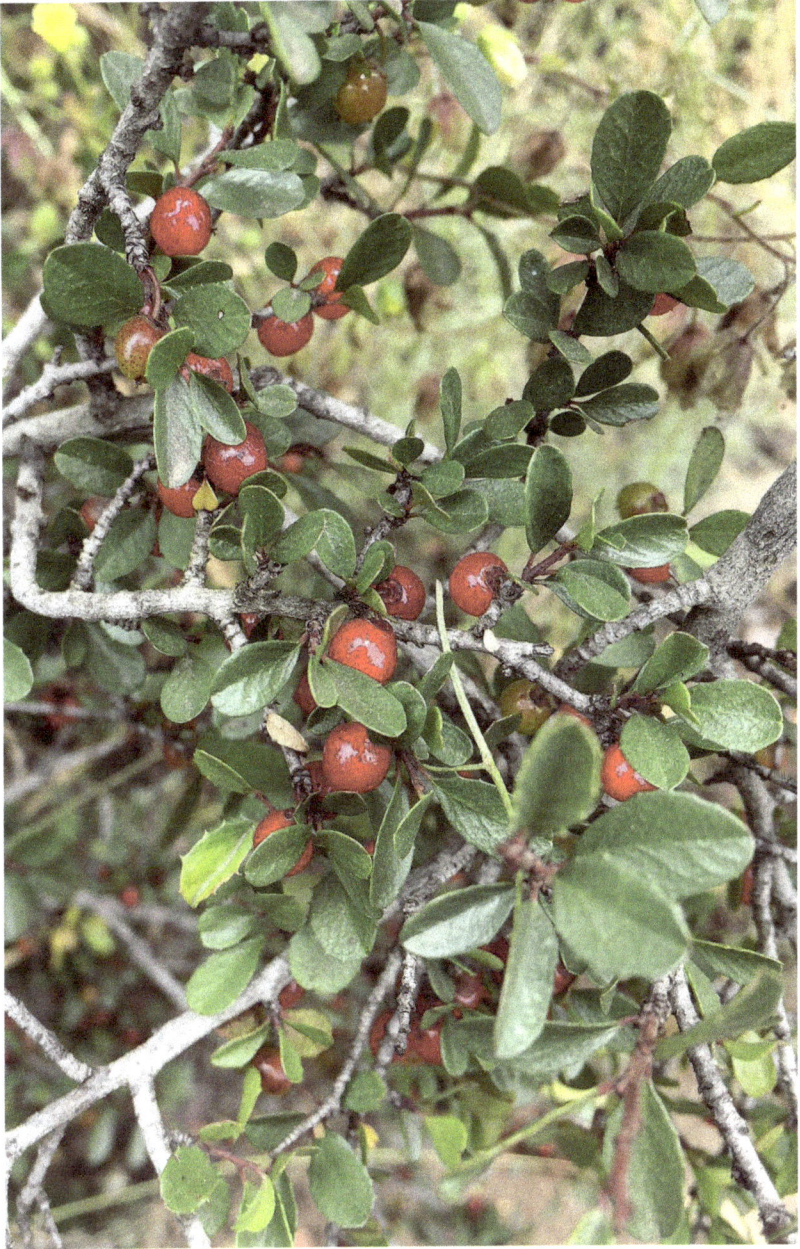

# *Rhamnus ilicifolia* Kellogg
## HOLLYLEAF REDBERRY

**BUCKTHORN FAMILY** (Rhamnaceae)

**DESCRIPTION** Erect evergreen shrub, similar to **redberry** (*Rhamnus crocea*), but taller, to 4 m tall, young stems slightly pubescent, reddish with bark becoming gray. **Leaves** 1 to 4 cm long, 1 to 4 cm wide, spine-toothed margins or rarely entire, leaf darker above, somewhat pubescent above and below. **Flowers** March to May, clusters of tiny greenish **Flowers** almost always without petals. **Fruits**, red berry 3 to 5 mm across, much like **redberry** (*R. crocea*). Redberry and hollyleaf redberry often occur together.

**DISTRIBUTION** Up to 2000 m (6600 ft); chaparral to yellow pine forests or woodlands.

**FIRE RESPONSE** Stump-sprouts after fire.

**WILDLIFE VALUE** Probably same as **redberry** (*R. crocea*).

**CULTURAL VALUE** Probably same as **redberry** (*R. crocea*).

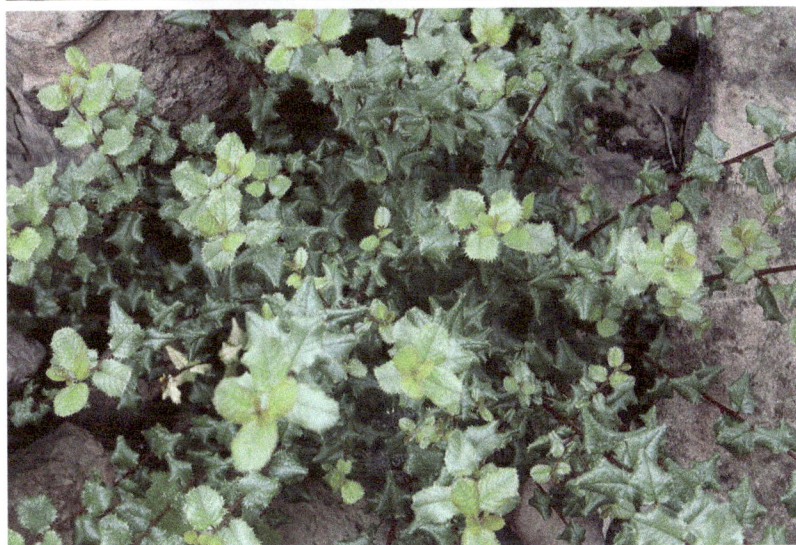

# Rhododendron occidentale (Torr. & Gray ex Torr.) Gray
## WESTERN AZALEA

**HEATH FAMILY** (Ericaceae)

**DESCRIPTION** Loosely branched deciduous shrub, 1 to 3 m tall, often branching 4 to 6 times in umbrella-like pattern, brown bark on young stems becoming gray and shreddy. **Leaves** simple, alternate, thin, light green, sometimes pubescent, midvein yellowish red and obvious, elliptic or obovate to oblanceolate, 3 to 9 cm long, 1.5 to 3.5 cm wide, stiff hairs along margins, lacking serration. **Flowers** May to July, showy, large, white or tinged pink. **Fruit**, capsule 1 to 2 cm long.

**DISTRIBUTION** Along streams, moist places, below 2300 m (7500 ft); mixed conifer, ponderosa or Jeffrey pine, willow.

**FIRE RESPONSE** Thicket-forming by lateral shoots.

**WILDLIFE VALUE** Toxic to cattle, sheep; much used by beaver.

**CULTURAL VALUE** None known.

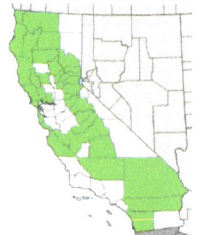

# *Rhododendron occidentale* (Torr. & Gray ex Torr.) Gray
## WESTERN AZALEA

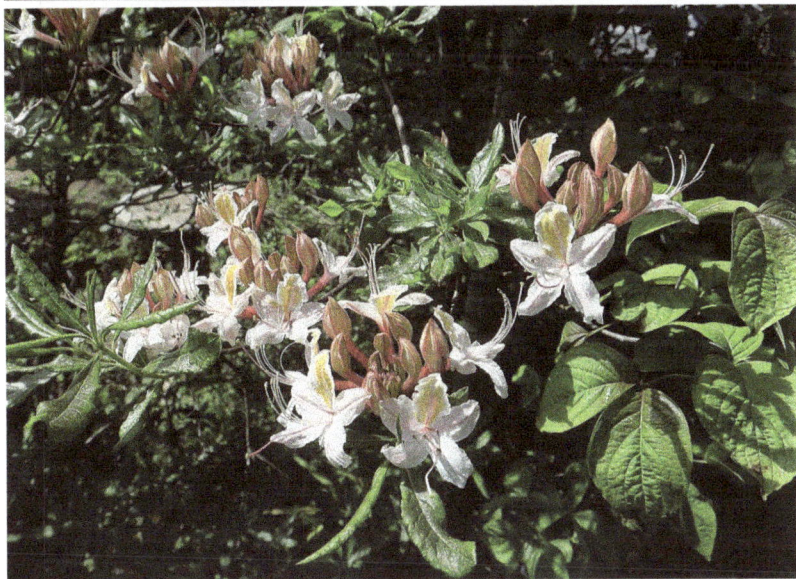

# *Rhus aromatica* Ait.
## SQUAW BUSH (BASKET SUMAC)

**SUMAC FAMILY** (Anacardiaceae)

**SYNONYM** *Rhus trilobata* Nutt.

**DESCRIPTION** Sprawling to erect normally deciduous shrub, stems to 1.5 m long, young twig ends tend to be reddish becoming gray with age, branches spreading and pubescent. **Leaves** 3-foliate, minutely hairy, leaflets may be pubescent ovate to obovate or almost diamond-shaped in outline with rounded serrations at apex, terminal 1 to 3 cm long, about as wide, terminal leaflet larger than laterals, lower margin concave taper to petiole, lower margin of lateral leaflets convex to petiole. **Flowers** March to May, yellowish clustered spikes. **Fruit**, reddish sticky, hairy drupe.

**DISTRIBUTION** Canyons and dry washes, below 1200 m (4000 ft); coastal sage scrub (soft chaparral), ceanothus chaparral, live oak and canyon live oak woodlands; southern California to Butte County.

**FIRE RESPONSE** Stump-sprouts after fire, cutting.

**WILDLIFE VALUE** Low value or staple browse for livestock, mule deer. Seeds eaten by quail, other birds.

**CULTURAL VALUE** Native Americans used stems in basket making. Berries used in several forms, food and medicine. Hopis used berry juice in body paint. Navajos made black dye from roots (Clarke 1977).

# *Rhus integrifolia* (Nutt.) Benth. & Hook. f. ex W.H. Brewer & S. Watson
## LEMONADEBERRY

**SUMAC FAMILY** (Anacardiaceae)

**DESCRIPTION** Rounded evergreen shrub, 1 to 3 m tall, fine fuzzy twigs and leaves. **Leaves** leathery, mid-vein prominent, flat, smooth margins or irregularly toothed, sometimes with curled down edges, 2.5 to 6 cm long, 1 to 4 cm wide, petiole 3 to 4 mm long, elliptic and rounded at both ends, glaucous to fuzzy with pubescence on veins at least, dark green above and paler below. **Flowers** January to March, white or pink oval clusters. **Fruit**, reddish and some-hat flattened, waxy drupe.

**DISTRIBUTION** Ocean bluffs, canyons below 600 m (2000 ft); inland to west Riverside County, Santa Barbara to Baja California.

**FIRE RESPONSE** Roots from branches touching ground; stump sprouts after fire, cutting.

**WILDLIFE VALUE** Low value browse; seed used by birds, including 8 to 9 percent of diet of roadrunners.

**CULTURAL VALUE** Fruits quite tart, yield a lemony drink when added to water. Cahuillas made tea of leaves to treat coughs and colds (Clarke 1977).

# *Rhus integrifolia* (Nutt.) Benth. & Hook. f. ex W.H. Brewer & S. Watson
## LEMONADEBERRY

# *Rhus ovata* S. Watson
## SUGAR BUSH

**SUMAC FAMILY** (Anacardiaceae)

**DESCRIPTION** Evergreen shrub, 1.5 to 3 m tall, stout reddish, hairless twigs. **Leaves** shiny green, thick, leathery, smooth margins, midvein prominent, ovate to lance-olate, tapering to a point at apex, 4 to 8 cm long, 2 to 4 cm wide, petiole 1 to 1.5 cm long, cupped upwards at edges from midvein to form a trough, edges wavy. **Flowers** April and May before producing new growth, hence old inflorescences not on ends of branches, flower panicles often present long before **Flowers** 5-parted, pinkish white, dense panicle. **Fruit**, reddish, pubescent, acid-tasting, sticky drupe, 7 to 8 mm diameter, single stone; relatively frost resistant.

**DISTRIBUTION** Dry chaparral slopes, mostly 300 to 1700 m (1000–5700 ft); coastal sage scrub (soft chaparral, chaparral).

**FIRE RESPONSE** Stump-sprouts rapidly after fire, cutting.

**WILDLIFE VALUE** Low value browse. Flowers attract bees, other insects; fruits important for birds, many animals.

**CULTURAL VALUE** Berries dried, eaten fresh, or ground into flour; white sap on berries used as acid flavoring (Clarke 1977).

# *Rhus ovata* S. Watson
## SUGAR BUSH

# *Ribes* spp.
## CURRANTS and GOOSEBERRIES

**FUCHSIA-FLOWERED GOOSEBERRY** (*Ribes speciosum*)

**GOOSEBERRY FAMILY** (Grossulariaceae)

**DESCRIPTION** Erect or trailing shrubs, drought or winter deciduous or evergreen, with simple, alternate, palmately lobed **leaves** and leaf venation; stems armed with spines at nodes where leaves join the stem or without spines; several species with both spines and internode prickles. **Flowers** 5-parted, produce many-seeded berries, may be covered with prickles, otherwise edible. Munz (1974) listed 17 species of *Ribes* in southern California; 11 of these have spines, 6 have pubescent to prickle-covered fruits; seven species are included here.

**FIRE RESPONSE** Most species stump-sprout after fire, cutting.

**WILDLIFE VALUE** Most species provide fair to poor browse for deer, livestock, bighorn sheep. Most berries taken by birds, many mammals, insects.

**CULTURAL VALUE** Berries edible. Most serious problem is coat of prickles that encase berries of some species. According to Clarke (1974), currants and goose-berries important ingredients in pemmican, an important part of diet of Native Americans.

**BITTER GOOSEBERRY** (*Ribes amarum*)

*Key to Ribes*

**1a**. Stems with spines at nodes.

    **2a**. Stems usually with bristles or prickles between nodes.

        **3a**. Leaves sticky; straggling shrub on dry pine woodland slopes above 2100 m elevation.........**MOUNTAIN GOOSEBERRY**, *R. montigenum*

        **3b**. Leaves not sticky; spreading shrub in shaded moist coast sage and chaparral canyons below 450 m elevation. ........................
................**FUCHSIA-FLOWERED GOOSEBERRY**, *R. speciosum*

    **2b**. Stems without bristles or prickles between nodes.

        **4a**. Leaves more or less equally pubescent on both surfaces; erect shrub on shady, moist woodland slopes below 1800 m. ..................
...............................**BITTER GOOSEBERRY**, *R. amarum*

        **4b**. Leaves darker green and less pubescent above; spreading shrub on dry chaparral to conifer slopes between 1100 and 2600 m...........
...........................**CHAPARRAL GOOSEBERRY**, *R. roezlii*

**1b**. Stems without spines at nodes.

    **5a**. Young stems covered with woolly and/or gland-tipped bristly hairs; multiple stemmed shrub common on dry chaparral and woodland slopes below 1500 m. .......................**CHAPARRAL CURRANT**, *R. malvaceum*

    **5b**. Young stems glabrous or with fine puberulence.

        **6a**. Leaves rather thin and flexible, somewhat paler and more pubescent below; slender stemmed shrub of moist places between 900 and 3000 m..........................**SIERRA CURRANT**, *R. nevadense*

        **6b**. Leaves somewhat stiff and leathery, color and pubescents nearly equal above and below; erect shrub in moist places in scrub oak chaparral and oak woodlands below 500 m............................
....................**GOLDEN CURRANT**, *R. aureum* var. *gracillimum*

# *Ribes amarum* McClatchie
## BITTER GOOSEBERRY

**GOOSEBERRY FAMILY** (Grossulariaceae)

**DESCRIPTION** Erect, drought-deciduous shrub, 1 to 2 m tall, brown nodal spines, lacking prickles on rest of stems, young stems pubescent. **Leaves** pubescent to somewhat glandular-puberulent on both surfaces roundish to palmate, heart-shaped at base, darker green above, 1.5 to 3 cm wide, petiole to 3 cm long, 3- to 5-lobed with rounded serrations, leaves develop in January and February. **Flowers** February to April, 1 to 3 on pubescent peduncles, blossoms purplish. **Fruit**, berry, 1.5 to 2 cm diameter, densely covered with gland-tipped bristles.

**DISTRIBUTION** Shady, usually moist wooded slopes below 1800 m (6000 feet).

**FIRE RESPONSE** Resprouts after burning, cutting.

**WILDLIFE VALUE** Low value browse, fruit eaten by many animals.

**CULTURAL VALUE** Edible berries well armed (see Clarke 1974).

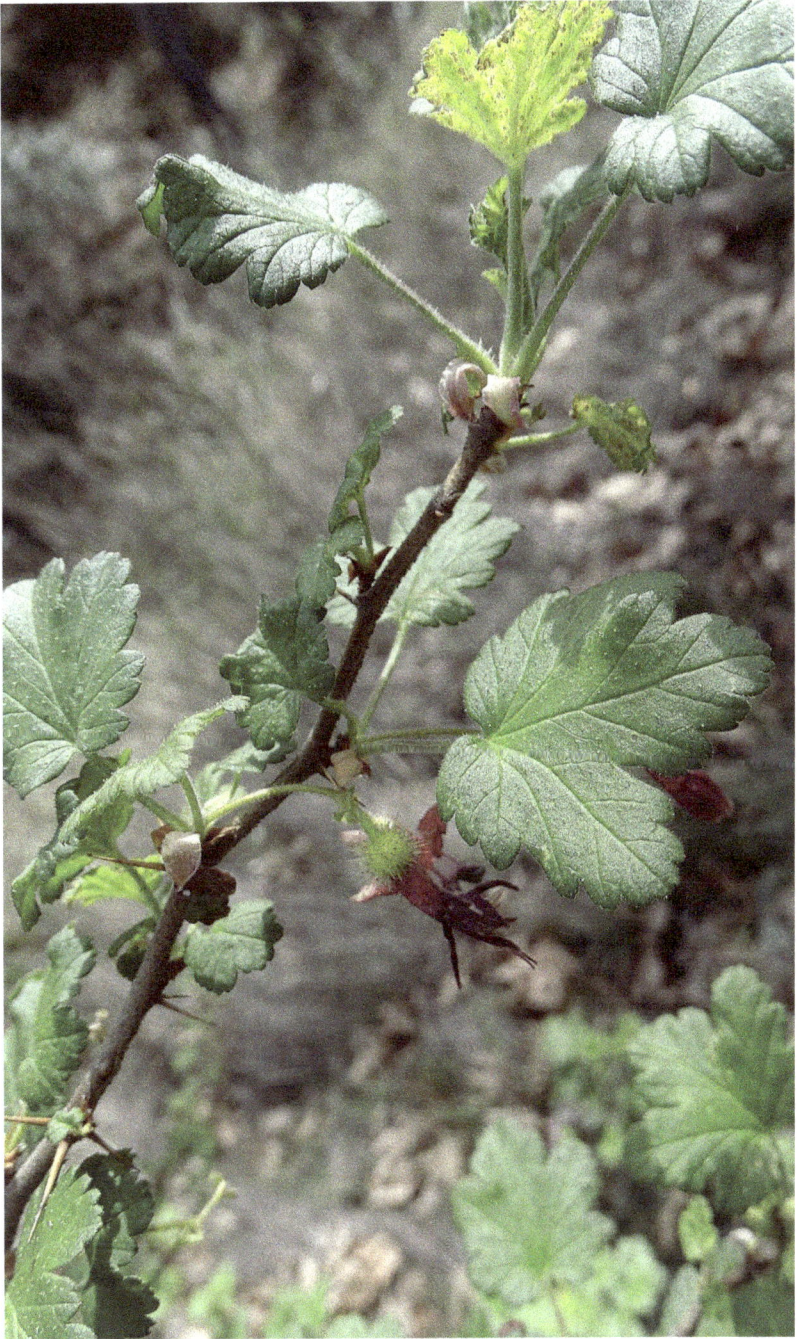

# *Ribes aureum* Pursh **var. *gracillimum*** (Coville & Britt.) Jepson
## GOLDEN CURRANT

**GOOSEBERRY FAMILY** (Grossulariaceae)

**DESCRIPTION** Erect, drought-deciduous shrub, bark gray or brown, 1 to 2 m tall, stems without spines, young stems and leaves nearly glabrous. **Leaves** fairly stiff, leathery, mostly 3-lobed, light green with palmate venation, lobes rounded or toothed, 2 to 5 cm long, 1.5 to 5 cm wide, petioles 1 to 4 cm long. **Flowers** January to June, 5 to 15 odorless yellow blossoms becoming red, 5-parted, 3- to 7-cm long raceme. **Fruit**, berry 6 to 8 mm diameter without bristles, mostly orange to yellowish or black, fruit color sometimes varies on same plant.

**DISTRIBUTION** Moist places on foothill areas below 500 m (1650 ft); scrub oak chaparral and oak woodland.

**FIRE RESPONSE** Sprout after cutting, fire.

**WILDLIFE VALUE** Low value browse; fruit eaten by numerous species.

**CULTURAL VALUE** Tasty berry used fresh, in cooking; probably used by Native Americans in several ways, an ingredient of pemmican (Clarke 1977).

# *Ribes aureum* Pursh **var. *gracillimum*** (Coville & Britt.) Jepson
## GOLDEN CURRANT

# *Ribes malvaceum* Sm.
## CHAPARRAL CURRANT

**GOOSEBERRY FAMILY** (Grossulariaceae)

**DESCRIPTION** drought-deciduous shrub, 1 to 2 m tall, 5 to 20 straight stout stems from base; young stems covered with woolly and gland-tipped bristly hairs. **Leaves** roundish in outline, 3- to 5-lobed, palmate venation, wrinkled surface, dull green above with stalked glands, margins serrate, paler green and pubescent below, 2 to 6 cm long and wide, petioles 1 to 5 cm long. **Flowers** December to April, 10 to 25 rose-colored blossoms in drooping terminal racemes, corolla tubular and abruptly flaring at apex, 8 to 12 mm long tube. **Fruit**, purplish-black berry, 6 mm diameter, somewhat hairy and glandular.

**SIMILAR SPECIES** Var. *viridifolium* Abrams has greener leaves and more coarse glandular pubescence; *Ribes indecorum* Eastw. similar with white flowers; *Ribes cereum* Douglas has more finely toothed leaves, found in San Gabriel Mountains, on Mt. Pinos.

**DISTRIBUTION** Common foothill shrub of dry places, several chaparral communities, oak woodlands, closed cone pine communities, mostly below 1500 m (5000 ft); San Jacinto Mountains to Santa Ana, Santa Monica Mountains.

**FIRE RESPONSE** Same as genus.

**WILDLIFE VALUE** See *R. aureum* var. *gracillimum.*

**CULTURAL VALUE** See *R. aureum* var. *gracillimum.*

# *Ribes montigenum* McClatchie
## MOUNTAIN GOOSEBERRY

**GOOSEBERRY FAMILY** (Grossulariaceae)

**DESCRIPTION** Low, straggling, much branched, drought-deciduous shrub, 0.3 to 0.6 m tall, usually bristly all along stems (sometimes almost smooth). **Leaves** glandular, sticky, appear round in outline, heart-shaped base, 1 to 4 cm long and wide, 5-cleft with much incised and toothed lobes, palmate venation, spines at base of petioles. **Flowers** July and August, 3 to 7 saucer-shaped blooms, short purplish to greenish white raceme. **Fruit**, bristly red berry about 6 mm diameter.

**DISTRIBUTION** Dry rocky places, 2100 to 3800 m (7000–12,500 ft); alpine and limber pine communities; San Jacinto, San Bernardino, San Gabriel Mountains to British Columbia, Rocky Mountains.

**FIRE RESPONSE** Variable root-sprouter after fire, cutting.

**WILDLIFE VALUE** Berries edible.

**CULTURAL VALUE** Fresh berries good raw, mashed and strained through sieve to remove bristles (Clarke 1977).

# *Ribes montigenum* McClatchie
## MOUNTAIN GOOSEBERRY

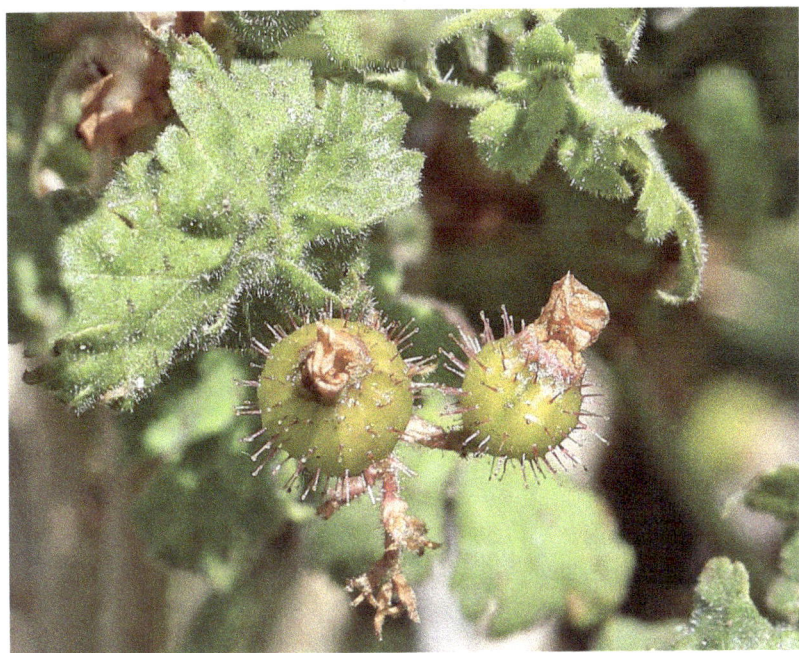

# *Ribes nevadense* Kellogg
## SIERRA CURRANT

**GOOSEBERRY FAMILY** (Grossulariaceae)

**DESCRIPTION** Slender stemmed, drought-deciduous shrub, 1 to 2 m tall, without spines or prickles, young growth glabrous or puberulent. **Leaves** roundish, rather thin and flexible, palmately 3- to 5-lobed, lobes obtuse, bluntly toothed, resinous-dotted and glabrous above, somewhat pubescent and paler below, 3 to 9 cm long and wide, petioles 1 to 6 cm long. **Flowers** April to July, drooping 8- to 12-flowered racemes, blossoms tubular and abruptly flaring at ends, tube approximately 5 mm long, small white petals with erect pink rose to red sepals. **Fruit**, blue black somewhat glandular, glaucous berry about 8 mm diameter.

**DISTRIBUTION** Moist places, stream sides; 900 to 3000 m (3000–10,000 ft); Palomar, San Gabriel, San Bernardino, and San Jacinto Mountains, north to Sierra Nevadas, Shasta and Modoc counties.

**FIRE RESPONSE** Resprouts when burned, cut.

**WILDLIFE VALUE** Berries eaten, especially by birds.

**CULTURAL VALUE** Berries edible (Clarke 1977).

# *Ribes roezlii* Regel
## CHAPARRAL GOOSEBERRY

**GOOSEBERRY FAMILY** (Grossulariaceae)

**DESCRIPTION** Drought-deciduous shrub, 0.5 to 1.2 m tall, long spreading stems and short rigid branchlets, 1 to 3 straight or recurved spines at leaf nodes. **Leaves** round in outline with palmate venation, 1.5 to 3.5 cm long and wide on 0.6 to 2 cm petiole, dark green with fine, short pubescence above, paler below, cleft into 3 to 5 lobes. **Flowers** April to July, 1 to 2 glandular, purplish red blooms with whitish petals, 3 to 5 mm long. **Fruit**, purple or sometimes pinkish or yellowish berry, 1.4 to 1.6 cm diameter, covered with stout spines, usually with some gland-tipped bristles.

**DISTRIBUTION** Dry slopes 1100 to 2600 m (3500–8500 ft); ponderosa or Jeffrey pine, bigcone Douglas-fir woodlands or forests, manzanita chaparral.

**FIRE RESPONSE** Stump-sprouts after fire, cutting.

**WILDLIFE VALUE** Staple browse for deer and bighorn sheep; fruit eaten by birds and small mammals.

**CULTURAL VALUE** Berries dried and stored or eaten raw.

246

# *Ribes speciosum* Pursh
## FUCHSIA-FLOWERED GOOSEBERRY

**GOOSEBERRY FAMILY** (Grossulariaceae)

**DESCRIPTION** Evergreen shrub, 1 to 2 m tall, spreading bristly branches, stems with three nodal spines 1 to 2 cm long. **Leaves** roundish to obovate with palmate venation, 1 to 3.5 cm long and wide, petiole 6 to 25 mm long, glossy dark green above, paler below, 3- to 5-lobed. **Flowers** January to May, 1 to 4 drooping, crimson, peduncled blossoms with stamens extending three times the length of petals. **Fruit**, bristly, glandular, oval-shaped berry about 1 cm long.

**DISTRIBUTION** Shaded, moist canyons below 500 m (1500 ft); coastal sage scrub (soft chaparral), chaparral.

**FIRE RESPONSE** Same as genus.

**WILDLIFE VALUE** Berries and flowers used by insects, birds, small animals.

**CULTURAL VALUE** Edible berries armed with bristles; colorful shrub useful as an ornament (McMinn 1964).

# *Ricinus communis* L.
## CASTOR-BEAN

**SPURGE FAMILY** (Euphorbiaceae)

**DESCRIPTION** Monoecious subshrub, to 3 m tall; young stems green or reddish or becoming reddish then brown, older stems have a ring at each leaf scar, easily identified by its large **leaves**, 10 to 30 cm long, 10 to 40 cm broad, prominately palmate 5- to 11-veined and lobed, glossy, lighter green below. **Flowers** most of year, inconspicuous clusters of blooms with female flowers higher on stem than male. **Fruit**, spiny capsule.

**DISTRIBUTION** Native of Old World, escaped from cultivation around arroyos, waste places up to 730 m (2000 ft).

**FIRE RESPONSE** Rather flammable, non-sprouter.

**WILDLIFE VALUE** Low value, toxic in large quantities.

**CULTURAL VALUE** Seeds more poisonous than leaves. Seeds ground into salve for sores; source of castor oil. This species was not available to Native Americans.

# *Ricinus communis* L.
## CASTOR-BEAN

# *Romneya coulteri* Harvey
## MATILIJA POPPY

**POPPY FAMILY** (Papaveraceae)

**DESCRIPTION** Subshrub with numerous wand-like green stems becoming gray with age and with clear bitter juice, from woody base, to 2.5 m tall. **Leaves** simple, sometimes sparsely toothed, alternate, olive-colored, lighter below, divided into 3 to 5 pinnate lobes, sometimes nearly separate, appear as leaflets, venation is pinnate, leaf 5 to 20 cm long, 5 to 15 cm wide, petiole 1 to 2 cm long. **Flowers** May to August, white and showy with crinkled petals 5 to 10 cm long. **Fruit**, capsule 3 to 4 cm long. Hybridizes with *R. trichocalyx* Eastw.

**DISTRIBUTION** Dry washes, canyons, below 1200 m (4000 ft); coastal sage scrub (soft chaparral) and chaparral.

**FIRE RESPONSE** Sprouts readily from underground roots.

**WILDLIFE VALUE** Low value.

**CULTURAL VALUE** Watery sap may have been used as a drink.

# *Rosa* spp.
## ROSES

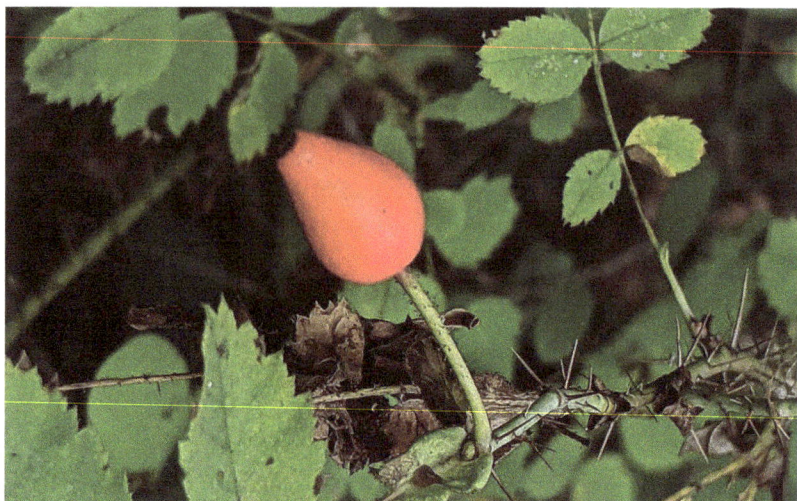

**WOOD ROSE** (*Rosa gymnocarpa*)

**ROSE FAMILY** (Rosaceae)

**DESCRIPTION** Erect or sprawling prickly shrubs. **Leaves** alternate, deciduous or almost evergreen, compound, with 5 to 7 leaflets arranged pinnately on leaf petiole. Ear-like appendices (stipules) at base of petioles are attached to stem along sides of petiole. Stem prickles in species included here may be straight or recurved. **Flower**, spring and summer, rose pink to red, may be borne singly or in cluster on floral stems.

**ADDITIONAL SPECIES** Munz (1974) listed three species in southern California; two are included here, most common below 1800 m (6000 ft). A third species, *R. woodsii* Lindl., with several high mountain and desert slope variations which are difficult to separate from *R. gymnocarpa* (since all have straight, slender prickles). *R. gymnocarpa* fruit easily identified because flower parts shed (and not persistent) from the rose hip fruit.

**DISTRIBUTION** Throughout region in moist and often more or less shaded areas.

**FIRE RESPONSE** Most species resprout from basal organs.

**WILDLIFE VALUE** Useful as food, cover.

**CULTURAL VALUE** Most rose species used for numerous purposes, especially as source of minerals and vitamin C.

*Key to Rosa*

**1a**. Stem prickles usually stout and recurved; erect shrub in moist places associated with willows and other riparian communities below 1800 m. . . . . . . . . . . . .
. . . . . . . . . . . . . . . . . . . . . . . . . . . . . . **CALIFORNIA WILD ROSE**, *R. californica*

**1b**. Stem prickles mostly slender and straight; slender shrub in moist shaded woodlands below 1500 m. . . . . . . . . . . . . . . . . . . . . . **WOOD ROSE**, *R. gymnocarpa*

**CALIFORNIA WILD ROSE** (*Rosa californica*)

# *Rosa californica* Cham. & Schlecht.
## CALIFORNIA WILD ROSE

**ROSE FAMILY** (Rosaceae)

**DESCRIPTION** Erect, branched, 1 3 m tall, young stems greenish with short prickles, stems become reddish brown and armed with stout recurved thorns. **Leaves** compound, divided into 5 to 7 leaflets; leaflets green, nearly oval, serrate, few scattered hairs to clearly pubescent, 1 to 5 cm long, wedge-shaped appendages (stipules) at base of leaf. **Flowers** April through August, rose-colored or pink, few to 30 in showy clusters, petals 1 to 2.5 cm long, ovary below sepals. **Fruit**, bright orange rose hip, 8 to 16 mm long, 10 to 15 mm thick.

**DISTRIBUTION** Moist places, canyons, near streams, below 1800 m (6000 ft); willow and other riparian plant communities.

**FIRE RESPONSE** Roots from branchlets, suckers; stump-sprouts after fire, cutting.

**WILDLIFE VALUE** Fruits staple for birds.

**CULTURAL VALUE** Hips and flowers used in tea as source of vitamin C, calcium, phosphorus, iron (Clarke 1977).

# *Rosa californica* Cham. & Schlecht.
## CALIFORNIA WILD ROSE

# *Rosa gymnocarpa* Nutt.
## WOOD ROSE

**ROSE FAMILY** (Rosaceae)

**DESCRIPTION** Slender shrub mostly 1 m tall or less, reddish-brown stems armed with slender straight prickles, numerous bristles. **Leaves** green, with stipules at base of petioles adherent to petiole stems, petiole up to 9 cm long including 5 to 7 leaflets nearly oval to roundish, leaflets 1 to 2.5 cm long, 0.6 to 1.2 cm wide with serrated margins commonly with glands on tips of teeth, glabrous and equal color on both surfaces. **Flowers** May to July, mostly solitary at ends of branchlets, red petals, ovary below sepals, ovary and sepals nearly glabrous. **Fruit**, reddish rose hip; as hip matures, sepals and other flower parts dry and fall away, leaving naked rose hip.

**DISTRIBUTION** In more or less moist shaded woods below 1500 m (5000 ft); Palomar and San Gabriel Mountains.

**FIRE RESPONSE** Probably resprouts following fire, cutting.

**WILDLIFE VALUE** Poor browse. **Flowers** and hips important staple for birds, animals, insects.

**CULTURAL VALUE** Rose hips an important source of vitamin C, calcium, phosphorus, and iron. Native Americans used roots, hips, and flowers (Clarke 1977).

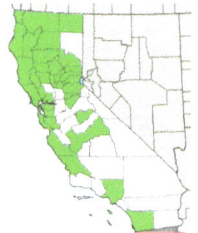

## Rosa gymnocarpa Nutt.
### WOOD ROSE

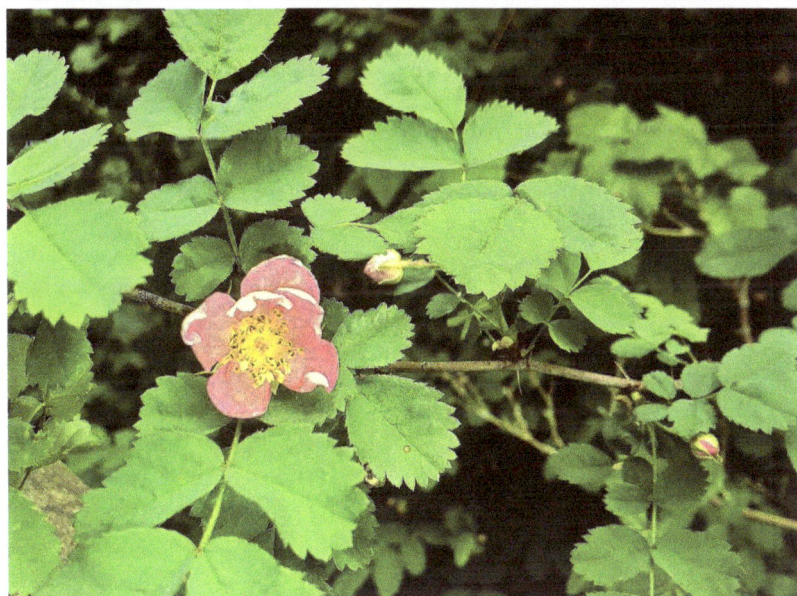

# *Rubus* spp.
## BLACKBERRIES

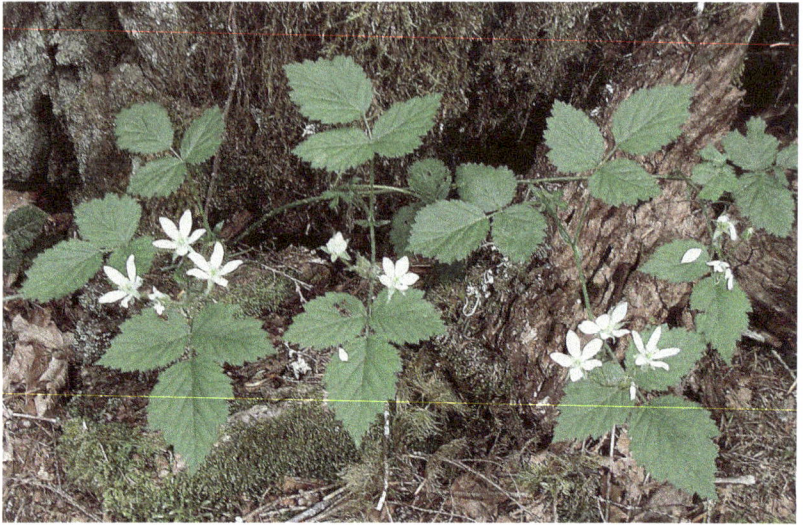

**CALIFORNIA BLACKBERRY** (*Rubus ursinus*)

**ROSE FAMILY** (Rosaceae)

**DESCRIPTION** Trailing or erect shrubs with or without spines and bristles. **Leaves** alternate, simple, or compound; if compound, generally 3 to 5 parted. First year canes normally do not produce flowers; in second year, flowers appear and foliage may appear different. Stipules at base of petioles adnate (connected) to petioles. **Flowers** 5-parted, usually white or pink or sometimes red solitary or in small clusters. **Fruit**s, many druplets crowded on elevated receptical.

**ADDITIONAL SPECIES** Munz (1974) listed seven species in southern California, three of which are included here. Three other species which Munz listed have escaped from cultivation; the fourth, *R. glaucifolious* Kellogg, Munz identified from shaded woods and coniferous forests on Palomar and Cuyamaca Mountains in San Diego County at 1400 to 1650 m (4500–5500 ft). Of the following species, the above is most easily confused with western raspberry (*R. leucodermis*), but stems of western raspberry more densely covered with prickles.

*Key to Rubus*

**1a**. Stems without prickles or spines, unarmed; common shrub in open conifer woodlands. . . . . . . . . . . . . . . . . . . . . . . . . . . . . . . **THIMBLEBERRY**, *R. parviflorus*
**1b**. Stems with prickles.

> **2a**. Leaves and petioles (stalk) with prickle-like pubescence; common shrub in many plant communities below 900 m. . . . . . . . . . . . . . . . . . . . . . . . . . . . . .
> . . . . . . . . . . . . . . . . . . . . . . . . . . . . . **CALIFORNIA BLACKBERRY**, *R. ursinus*
> **2b**. Leaves without prickles; leaf petioles (stalks) and stems with relatively few prickles; shrub in yellow pine woodlands. . . . . . . . . . . . . . . . . . . . . . . . . . .
> . . . . . . . . . . . . . . . . . . . . . . . . . . . . **WESTERN RASPBERRY**, *R. leucodermis*

**THIMBLEBERRY** (*Rubus parviflorus*)

# *Rubus leucodermis* Dougl. ex Torr. & Gray
## WESTERN RASPBERRY

**ROSE FAMILY** (Rosaceae)

**DESCRIPTION** Straggly shrub with trailing, prickly stems, some recurved prickles, arched and branched, may root at tips, brambles 1 to 2 m high. **Leaves** compound with 2 to 5 leaflets, whitish tomentum below, green above, prickly stalked, leaflets ovate to lanceolate, with terminal larger, 3 to 9 cm long, 1 to 5 cm wide, irregularly serrate. **Flowers** May to July, 3 to 10 blossoms in compact clusters, 5-petaled, white, 7 to 10 mm broad. **Fruit**, dark red to black raspberry, sweet, sometimes dry and abortive.

**DISTRIBUTION** Dry flats, slopes, 1400 to 2300 m (4700–7500 ft); yellow pine communities.

**FIRE RESPONSE** Root-sprouts after fire; spreads by rooting-branchlets.

**WILDLIFE VALUE** Fruits staple for game, birds, and small mammals.

**CULTURAL VALUE** Berries edible. Leaves can be dried, used for tea (Clarke 1977).

# *Rubus leucodermis* Dougl. ex Torr. & Gray
## WESTERN RASPBERRY

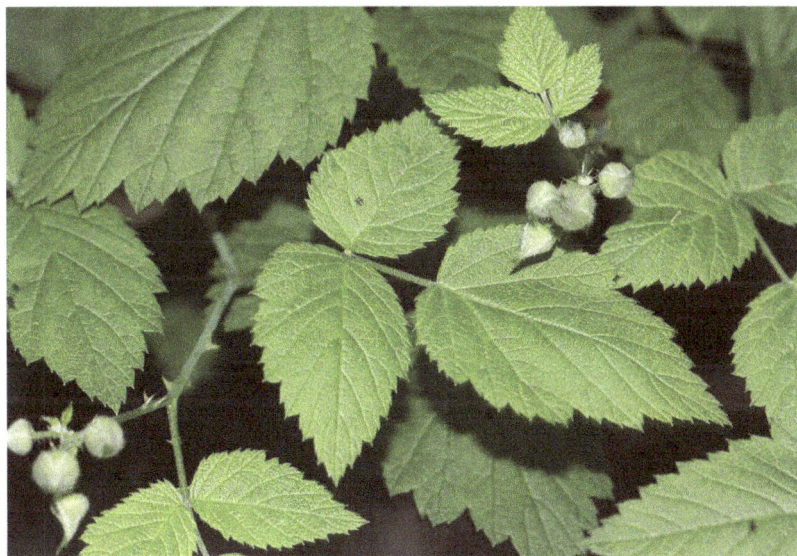

# *Rubus parviflorus* Nutt.
## THIMBLEBERRY

**ROSE FAMILY** (Rosaceae)

**DESCRIPTION** Low, scrambling deciduous shrub, 1 to 2 m tall, without prickles. **Leaves** large, simple, palmately 5-lobed, 9 to 13 cm long, 10 to 16 cm broad, unequally serrate, green with soft pubescence to tomentose on both surfaces, more so below. **Flowers** March through August, blooms 2 to 5 cm broad, few-flowered clusters, white petals 1.5 to 2 cm long. **Fruit**, dull red berry, somewhat like a blunt strawberry, 1 to 1.6 cm broad.

**DISTRIBUTION** Open woods and canyons, below 2400 m (8000 ft); yellow pine, mixed conifer, white fir woodlands or forests.

**FIRE RESPONSE** Sprouts from underground roots after fire, cutting.

**WILDLIFE VALUE** Berries staple food of many birds and mammals; low value browse.

**CULTURAL VALUE** Berries eaten raw or dried and stored, or used as ingredient in pemmican. Young shoots can be eaten fresh or boiled (Clarke 1977).

## *Rubus parviflorus* Nutt.
## THIMBLEBERRY

# *Rubus ursinus* Cham. & Schlecht.
## CALIFORNIA BLACKBERRY

**ROSE FAMILY** (Rosaceae)

**DESCRIPTION** Evergreen trailing or climbing shrub with many densely prickled stems, somewhat prickly leaves, young stems greenish becoming brown. **Leaves** green, lighter below, pubescent above, nearly tomentose below, mostly 3-parted on bristly stalks, leaf sometimes not compound but palmate-shaped, leaflets mostly ovate to oval, 2.5 to 12 cm long, 2 to 7 cm wide. **Flowers** March through July, white blooms 2 to 3 cm across, few to several flowered clusters near end of leafy branchlets. **Fruit**, sweet, black, somewhat bristly blackberry, to 2 cm long.

**DISTRIBUTION** Below 900 m (3000 ft); many plant communities.

**FIRE RESPONSE** Sprouts from suckers after fire, cutting.

**WILDLIFE VALUE** Fruits, important food of birds and animals.

**CULTURAL VALUE** Fruits, edible. Roots boiled with water to relieve diarrhea. Half-ripe berries soaked in water to make a drink, leaves used for tea (Clarke 1977).

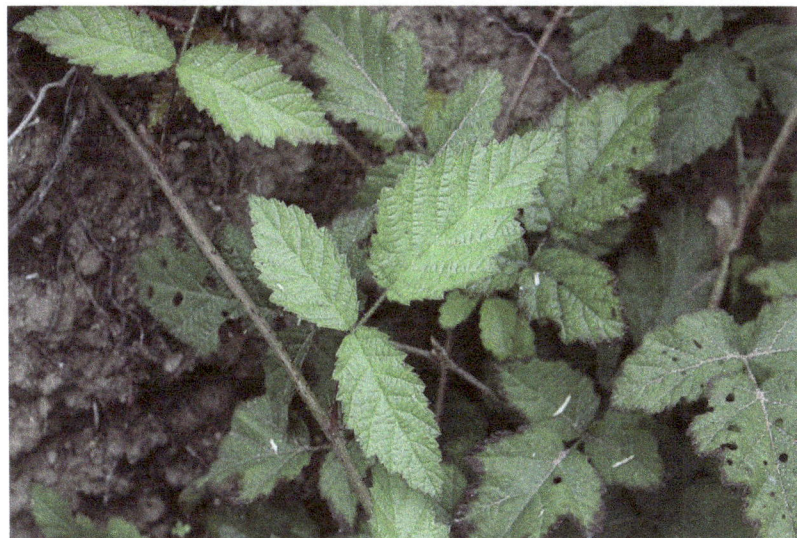

# *Salix* spp.
## WILLOWS

**ARROYO WILLOW** (*Salix lasiolepis*)

**WILLOW FAMILY** (Salicaceae)

**DESCRIPTION** Erect, dioecious shrubs to large trees with simple, alternate, deciduous leaves commonly associated with moist places. **Flowers** are single sex; on separate plants and borne in compact clusters called catkins. Male and female flowers are on separate plants. **Leaves** often start growing after plants flowered and are usually long and relatively narrow; leaves tend to end in gradually tapering tip or base. Often, one end of leaf is abrupt, the other tapered. Munz (1974) listed nine shrub willows; only two are included here. Two species listed below commonly occur below 2100 m (7000 ft) while remaining species tend to be rare below 1800 m (6000 ft) or are desert species.

### Key to Salix

**1a.** Bark gray and furrowed, young stems with gray hair; shrub or small tree along streams and other wet places. . **SANDBAR WILLOW**, *Salix exigua* var. *hindsiana*

**1b.** Bark smooth and dark brown to yellowish, twigs brownish to yellowish; shrub or small tree along streams and other wet places. . . . . . . . . . . . . . . . . . . . . . . . . . . . .
. . . . . . . . . . . . . . . . . . . . . . . . . . . . . . . . . . . . . . .**ARROYO WILLOW**, *S. lasiolepis*

**SANDBAR WILLOW** (*Salix exigua* var. *hindsiana*)

# *Salix exigua* var. *hindsiana* (Benth.) Dorn
## SANDBAR WILLOW

**WILLOW FAMILY** (Salicaceae)

**SYNONYM** *Salix hindsiana* Benth.

**DESCRIPTION** Erect, deciduous shrub or small tree, to 7 m tall, with gray, furrowed bark; young stems with dense gray-woolly hair. **Leaves** light green, simple, alternate, nearly linear, mostly 4 to 8 cm long, 0.2 to 1.6 cm wide, entire or with minute serrations or sometimes vaguely denticulate, mostly covered with gray, silky hairs, midvein with several laterals tending toward leaf tip. **Flowers** March to June, following leaf development in February and March. **Fruit**, 2-valved, silky to nearly glabrous capsule, almost sessile.

**SIMILAR SPECIES Narrowleaf willow**, *S. exigua* var. *exigua*, with leaves usually less hairy and greener above.

**DISTRIBUTION** Wet places, sandbars; common.

**FIRE RESPONSE** Root-sprouts after fire, cuttings.

**WILDLIFE VALUE** Staple browse for deer, preferred by livestock.

**CULTURAL VALUE** Leaves and green bark probably ground and steeped in water for use as beverage to relieve colds, headaches, etc. Salicylic acid, an active ingredient of aspirin, first isolated in Europe from a *Salix*.

# *Salix exigua* var. *hindsiana* (Benth.) Dorn
## SANDBAR WILLOW

# *Salix lasiolepis* Benth.
## ARROYO WILLOW

**WILLOW FAMILY** (Salicaceae)

**DESCRIPTION** Erect, deciduous shrub or small tree, 2 to 10 m tall, smooth bark and yellowish to dark brown twigs. **Leaves** simple, alternate, wider above the middle than below, oblanceolate or obovate, leaf size highly variable, 2 to 10 cm long, 0.6 to 3 cm wide, sometimes serrate, flat to rolled under at edges, green and hairless above, pubescent and white-filmy below. **Flowers** February to April (usually before, but sometimes coincidental with leaf development) in slender, compact clusters (catkins), dark scales. **Fruit**, 2-valved, glabrous or finely pubescent, pedicled capsule.

**DISTRIBUTION** Stream banks, sandbars, other wet places below 2100 m (7000 ft); many plant communities; throughout cismontane California, occasional on desert side.

**FIRE RESPONSE** Stump-sprouts and root-sprouts after fire, cutting.

**WILDLIFE VALUE** Staple or preferred browse of deer, bighorn sheep, and beaver.

**CULTURAL VALUE** Leaves ground and steeped for several hours; beverage used to relieve colds, headaches, and other pains.

## *Salix lasiolepis* Benth.
### ARROYO WILLOW

# *Salvia* spp.
SAGE

**WHITE SAGE** (*Salvia apiana*)

**MINT FAMILY** (Lamiaceae)

*Key to Salvia*

**1a**. Leaves green to grayish green, at least above.

    **2a**. Leaves dark green and wrinkled above; shrub, foothills in coastal sage scrub to chamise chaparral. ................**BLACK SAGE**, *S. mellifera*

    **2b**. Leaves grayish green and wrinkled on both surfaces; occasional shrub in chamise chaparral and coastal sage scrub in San Diego County.........
    ....................................**CLEVELAND SAGE**, *S. clevelandii*

**1b**. Leaves and stems whitish gray.

    **3a**. Plants generally coastal, below 600 m in coastal sage scrub. ..........
    ......................................**PURPLE SAGE**, *S. leucophylla*

    **3b**. Plants more interior, up to 1500 m in woodlands and sage scrub. .....
    .............................................**WHITE SAGE**, *S. apiana*

**PURPLE SAGE** (*Salvia leucophylla*)

# *Salvia apiana* Jepson
## WHITE SAGE

**MINT FAMILY** (Lamiaceae)

**DESCRIPTION** Subshrub, 1 to 2 m tall, very white on stems and leaves, long erect branches from base, young stems square. **Leaves** simple, opposite, canescent, crowded at base of branches, lanceolate with some rounded teeth on leaf margins, 3 to 9 cm long, 1 to 3.5 cm wide, petioles variable, leaves appear white with fuzzy texture. **Flowers** March to July, white to pale lavender, blooms in whorls at leaf axils in terminal, few flowered racemes 50 to 150 cm long, pedicels 3 to 15 cm long on opposite sides of stems. **Fruit**, 4 nutlets, 2.5 to 3 mm long, become separate at maturity.

**DISTRIBUTION** Widespread, mostly below 1500 m (5000 ft); yellow pine woodlands, sage scrub (soft chaparral), chamise chaparral.

**FIRE RESPONSE** Numerous root-sprouts and seedlings following fire.

**WILDLIFE VALUE** Low value browse mostly by rodents. Seeds taken by birds and rodents. Flowers preferred by bees.

**CULTURAL VALUE** Leaves used for tea, or in sweathouses to remove body odors before a hunt. Elongating stalks can be peeled and eaten.

# *Salvia clevelandii* (Gray) Greene
## CLEVELAND SAGE

**MINT FAMILY** (Lamiaceae)

**DESCRIPTION** Sweetly fragrant low shrub, to 1 m tall, young stems square and tomentose. **Leaves** grayish green covered with short hairs (canescent), somewhat wrinkled on both surfaces, dark green above, lighter below, elliptic-oblong with small rounded teeth on leaf margins, 1 to 5 cm long, 0.5 to 1.5 cm wide, petioles mostly 1 to 6 mm long. **Flowers** December through September, along elongated flowering stem in widely-spaced whorled clusters, blue violet to occasionally whitish. **Fruit**, 4 nutlets, 1.5 to 2 mm long, becoming separate at maturity.

**SIMILAR SPECIES** Appears somewhat like *Salvia mellifera,* but with grayer foliage, and has characteristic sweet fragrance.

**DISTRIBUTION** Below 1100 m (3000 ft); chamise chaparral to coastal sage scrub (soft chaparral).

**FIRE RESPONSE** Variable sprouter from roots and stems after cutting; rather flammable especially when flower stems mature and become dry.

**WILDLIFE VALUE** Low value browse.

**CULTURAL VALUE** Leaves excellent for tea or cooking.

# *Salvia leucophylla* Greene
## PURPLE SAGE

**MINT FAMILY** (Lamiaceae)

**DESCRIPTION** Much-branched shrub, 1 to 1.5 m tall, whitish stems, young stems square, reddish becoming gray with age. **Leaves** opposite with several secondary leaves at primary leaf node, primary leaves ovate to almost lance-shaped, 6 or 7 cm long, 0.5 to 2.5 cm wide, petioles (if present) 3 to 8 mm long, leaves with rounded teeth on margins, grayish green above with rough, wrinkled surface, paler and white, fuzzy below. **Flowers** April to June, lavender, 3 to 5 compact, whorled clusters on elongated flowering stems. **Fruit**, 4 nutlets, 3 to 4 mm long, separates at maturity.

**DISTRIBUTION** Coastal mountains below 600 m (2000 ft); coastal sage scrub (soft chaparral).

**FIRE RESPONSE** Root-sprouts after fire, cutting; rather flammable, especially when flower stems mature and become dry.

**WILDLIFE VALUE** Low value browse; seeds eaten by birds.

**CULTURAL VALUE** Can be used to make a pleasant herb tea.

# *Salvia mellifera* Greene
## BLACK SAGE

**MINT FAMILY** (Lamiaceae)

**DESCRIPTION** Shrub, 1 to 2 m tall, young stems square, hairy, sometimes purple, commonly greenish, become brownish gray with age. **Leaves** simple, opposite, mostly elliptic to oblong, dark green with many small crenate (rounded teeth) margins, wrinkled above, lighter to ash-colored below and covered with short hairs (canescent), 2 to 6 cm long, less than 1.5 cm wide, petioles (if present) 10 to 12 mm long. **Flowers** March to June, pale blue to whitish, 2-lipped, compact whorls, spaced along elongated stem. **Fruit**, 4 nutlets about 2 mm long, separates at maturity.

**DISTRIBUTION** Foothills below 900 m (3000 ft); coastal sage scrub (soft chaparral) to chamise chaparral.

**FIRE RESPONSE** Rather flammable, especially when flower stems mature and become dry; many root-sprouts and seedlings after fire.

**WILDLIFE VALUE** Browsed by rodents, low value; seeds staple of birds, small mammals. Flowers preferred by honey bees.

**CULTURAL VALUE** Seeds parched and ground into meal. Leaves and stalks used as condiment.

# *Sambucus nigra* ssp. *canadensis* (L.) R. Bolli
## MEXICAN ELDERBERRY

**MUSKROOT FAMILY** (Adoxaceae)

**SYNONYM** *Sambucus mexicana* C. Presl. ex DC.

**DESCRIPTION** Tall shrub or small tree, 2 to 8 m tall, young stems reddish becoming brown, old bark heavily ridged, thick and grayish. **Leaves** opposite, compound, divided into 3 or more (commonly 5, sometimes 7) leaflets, terminal leaflet 4 to 14 cm long, 2 to 5 cm wide, leaflets ovate to obovate, finely serrate and pubescent to glabrous. **Flowers** April through July, small blooms with five dull white petals in flat-topped spreading cluster, 4 to 10 cm across. **Fruit**, bluish drupe about 5 mm across, white filmy covering.

**SIMILAR SPECIES** **Blue elderberry** [*Sambucus nigra* ssp. *cerulea* (Raf.) R. Bolli] occurs at higher elevations to 3000 m (10,000 ft), 5 to 9 leaflets, better flavored berries.

**DISTRIBUTION** Common in canyons and valleys, below 1700 m (5600 ft); many plant communities.

**FIRE RESPONSE** Stump-sprouts after fire.

**WILDLIFE VALUE** Staple browse plant; fruits preferred by birds, small mammals, rodents.

**CULTURAL VALUE** Flower clusters dried, preserved, and later cooked to make sweet sauce. Berries eaten fresh or stored, used to make purple black dye. Stems used to make yellow or orange dye. Native Americans made flutes from branches and arrow shafts from straight stems (Sweet 1962).

# *Sambucus nigra* ssp. *canadensis* (L.) R. Bolli
## MEXICAN ELDERBERRY

# *Senecio flaccidus* var. *douglasii* (DC.) B.L. Turner & T.M. Barkley
## BUSH GROUNDSEL

**SUNFLOWER FAMILY** (Asteraceae)

**SYNONYM** *Senecio douglasii* DC.

**DESCRIPTION** Straggly or straight branched subshrub, 1 to 1.6 m tall, leafy up to **Flowers** young stems light green and tomentose becoming less tomentose and brown with age, mature bark gray, stems marked with longitudinal lines or furrows. **Leaves** 3 to 10 cm long, linear, filiform or divided into 5 to 9 linear lobes, upper leaves commonly 3-lobed or entire, leaf divisions usually deep enough to make leaf appear compound, divisions flattened and near filiform, gray green above, whitish fuzz below. **Flowers** April through November, several to many showy, yellow heads with 10 to 13 rays, 10 to 15 mm long. **Fruit**, hairy achene about 4 mm long.

**DISTRIBUTION** Common in washes, dry hillsides, below 1800 m (6000 ft); coastal sage scrub (soft chaparral) to scrub oak chaparral; coast ranges.

**FIRE RESPONSE** Information not available.

**WILDLIFE VALUE** Low value.

**CULTURAL VALUE** None known.

# *Senecio flaccidus* var. *douglasii* (DC.) B.L. Turner & T.M. Barkley
## BUSH GROUNDSEL

**ADDITIONAL SPECIES** *Senecio spartiodes* Torr. & Gray (not illustrated), of higher elevation, 2400 to 3200 m (8000–10,500 ft), from a thick woody base (caudex), stems leafy up to flowers; leaves mostly linear, entire, and glabrous, 3 to 10 cm long, 1.5 to 5 mm wide; flowers approximately same as *S. flaccidus,* blooming more pronounced in mid-summer.

# *Simmondsia chinensis* (Link) Schneid.
## JOJOBA (GOATNUT)

**BOX FAMILY** (Simmondsiaceae)

**NOTE** Family Simmondsiaceae not recognized by all taxonomic systems; the single species, *Simmondsia chinensis,* sometimes retained in family Buxaceae.

**DESCRIPTION** Rigid, spreading dioecious evergreen shrub, 1 to 2 m tall, young stems densely pubescent and green becoming gray. **Leaves** leathery, simple, opposite, approximately ovate, 2 to 5 cm long, 1.0 to 2.5 cm wide, petiole very short or absent, leaf surfaces about equally covered with fine pubescence, pale green or yellowish, 1- to 3-veined from base. **Flowers** March to May, male and female flowers on separate plants, pale green or yellowish, 3 to 4 mm long with sepals only, female flowers become 10 to 20 mm long as fruit develops. **Fruit**, smooth cylindrical capsule about 2 cm long, resembling an acorn.

**DISTRIBUTION** Dry barren slopes, below 1500 m (5000 ft); creosote bush, Joshua tree woodland; Little San Bernardino Mountains, west to Riverside, San Diego counties to Baja California.

**FIRE RESPONSE** Information not available.

**WILDLIFE VALUE** Fruits staple for small mammals, birds. Leaves and twigs staple browse for livestock.

**CULTURAL VALUE** Seeds eaten fresh or ground and mixed with water for coffee-like beverage (Clarke 1977). Oil from nut has considerable commercial value as whale oil substitute.

## *Simmondsia chinensis* (Link) Schneid.
### JOJOBA (GOATNUT)

Male jojoba plant with flowers (upper); female plant with fruit (lower).

# *Spartium junceum* L.
## SPANISH BROOM

**PEA FAMILY** (Fabaceae)

**DESCRIPTION** Tall broom-like drought-deciduous shrub, to 3 m tall, stems green becoming gray at base often nearly leafless. **Leaves** (when present) green, simple, alternate, entire and glabrous, oblong-oblanceolate, 1 to 3 cm long, 2 to 6 mm wide. **Flowers** April to June, bright yellow, 2 to 2.5 cm long, fragrant, terminal clusters on straight green stems. **Fruit**, pod 5 to 10 cm long.

**DISTRIBUTION** Frequent escapee from cultivation or planted along roadsides below 2100 m (7000 ft).

**FIRE RESPONSE** Information not available.

**WILDLIFE VALUE** Not used.

**CULTURAL VALUE** Introduced.

# *Styrax redivivus* (Torr.) L.C. Wheeler
## STORAX

**STORAX FAMILY** (Styracaceae)

**SYNONYM** *Styrax officinalis* L. var. *fulvescens* Eastw.

**DESCRIPTION** Erect, deciduous shrub to 4 m tall with grayish twigs, young stems pubescent. **Leaves** 2 to 9 cm long, 1.5 to 7 cm wide, upper surface pubescent, rather short brownish matted hair below, roundish (round-ovate to obovate), obtuse or subcordate base, obtuse to rounded apex, petioles to 10 mm long. **Flowers** April to May, terminal clusters of white blossoms with 4- to 10-lobed corolla, 12 to 18 mm long, persistent, unequally toothed calyx on flowering branchlets, peduncles 6 to 12 mm long. **Fruit**, globose-oval seed about 12 to 14 mm long.

**DISTRIBUTION** On slopes and in canyons to 1500 m (5000 ft); chaparral and southern oak woodlands.

**FIRE RESPONSE** Not known.

**WILDLIFE VALUE** Unknown.

**CULTURAL VALUE** None known.

# *Styrax redivivus* (Torr.) L.C. Wheeler
## STORAX

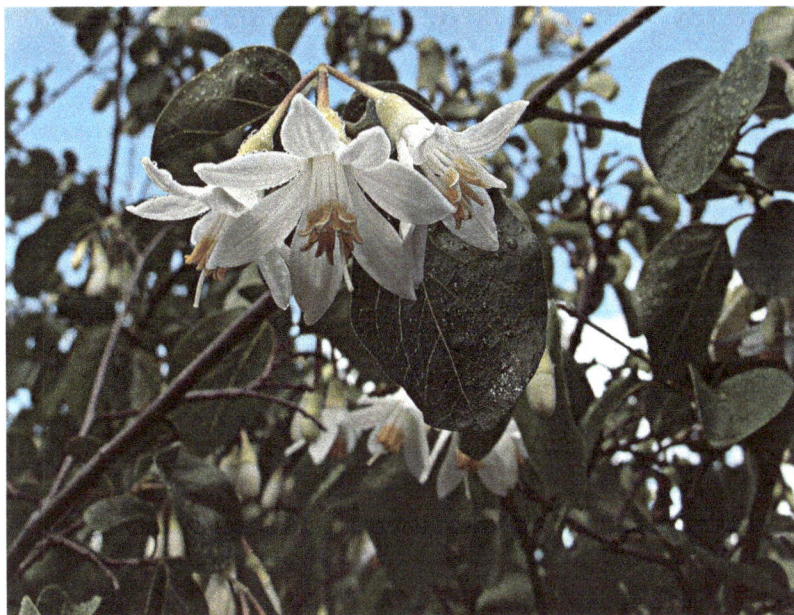

# *Symphoricarpos mollis* Nutt.
## SPREADING SNOWBERRY

**HONEYSUCKLE FAMILY** (Caprifoliaceae)

**DESCRIPTION** Low sprawling, deciduous shrub, stems to 90 cm long, twigs reddish, usually with dense short, curved hairs. **Leaves** opposite, grayish green to light green, oval to nearly ovate, usually entire, rarely lobed, short pubescence above and densely pubescent with whitish appearance beneath, 1 to 4 cm long, 0.7 to 3 cm wide. **Flowers** March through August, short clusters or pairs, corolla lobes pink, bell-shaped, 3 to 5 mm long, lobes 2 to 3 mm long. **Fruit**, white berry-like drupe (hence the name snowberry).

**DISTRIBUTION** Shaded slopes, below 900 m (3000 ft), sometimes to 1500 m (5000 ft); oak woodland, conifer forest, chaparral, scrub oak chaparral; coast ranges, Mendocino County to Baja California.

**FIRE RESPONSE** Sometimes roots at branchlet tips; stump sprouts after fire.

**WILDLIFE VALUE** Staple or preferred browse for deer, preferred browse of cattle and sheep. Honey bees use flowers.

**CULTURAL VALUE** Leaves contain saponin, possibly in poisonous amounts; Native Americans used portions of roots and fruits for medicinal purposes (Sweet 1962).

# *Symphoricarpos mollis* Nutt.
## SPREADING SNOWBERRY

**SIMILAR SPECIES Mountain snowberry**, *Symphoricarpos rotundifolius* var. *parishii* (Rydb.) Dempster (not illustrated), funnel-shaped, white yellow to pink flower; leaves thicker than *S. mollis,* grayish green on both surfaces; occurs at higher elevations 1500 to 3400 m (5000-11,000 ft) throughout San Bernardino National Forest to Humboldt County.

# *Tetradymia comosa* Gray
## HAIRY HORSEBRUSH

**SUNFLOWER FAMILY** (Asteraceae)

**DESCRIPTION** Erect bush, 0.5 to 1.2 m tall, white fuzzy (tomentose) branchlets, light gray, darkening to dark gray with patches of fuzzy scales; tomentose **leaves**, simple, entire, alternate, whitish, linear, 2.5 to 5 cm long, to 2 mm wide, early leaves flexible, later become rigid and spine-tipped, sometimes short leaves in fascicle with principle leaves. **Flowers** June to September, heads of 6 to 10 tube flowers (no ray flowers) subtended by 5 to 6 woolly bracts. **Fruit**, achene covered with long, woolly hairs.

**DISTRIBUTION** Dry places usually on interior mountain slopes, below 1500 m (5000 ft); coastal sage scrub (soft chaparral), chaparral and many other shrub plant communities; southern California, north to Newhall, occasional in Mojave Desert.

**FIRE RESPONSE** Stump-sprouts after fire.

**WILDLIFE VALUE** Low value.

**CULTURAL VALUE** None known.

# *Toxicodendron diversilobum* (Torr. & A. Gray) Greene
## POISON-OAK

**SUMAC FAMILY** (Anacardiaceae)

**DESCRIPTION** Erect or spreading deciduous shrub, 1 to 3 m tall, young stems olive green to reddish becoming dark brown and somewhat shreddy. **Leaves** 3-foliate, divisions with rounded serration or lobed, ovate to round in outline, leaflets 2 to 7 cm long, 1 to 5 cm wide, leaves bright green and shiny above, paler below, leaflets glabrous to more or less pubescent on veins, new leaves usually red. **Flowers** March through June, small, greenish white blossoms in drooping clusters from leaf axils. **Fruit**, white or brownish, berry-like drupe.

**DISTRIBUTION** Low places, thickets, stream banks, below 1500 m (5000 ft); many plant communities.

**FIRE RESPONSE** Root-sprouts.

**WILDLIFE VALUE** Fair to poor browse for deer and livestock

**CULTURAL VALUE** Oils from this species cause most people to break out with minor to serious allergic skin rash and swelling, may be more serious if taken internally. Reputedly, Native Americans were not allergic to the plant and used sap for black dye in basketry.

# *Toxicodendron diversilobum* (Torr. & A. Gray) Greene
## POISON-OAK

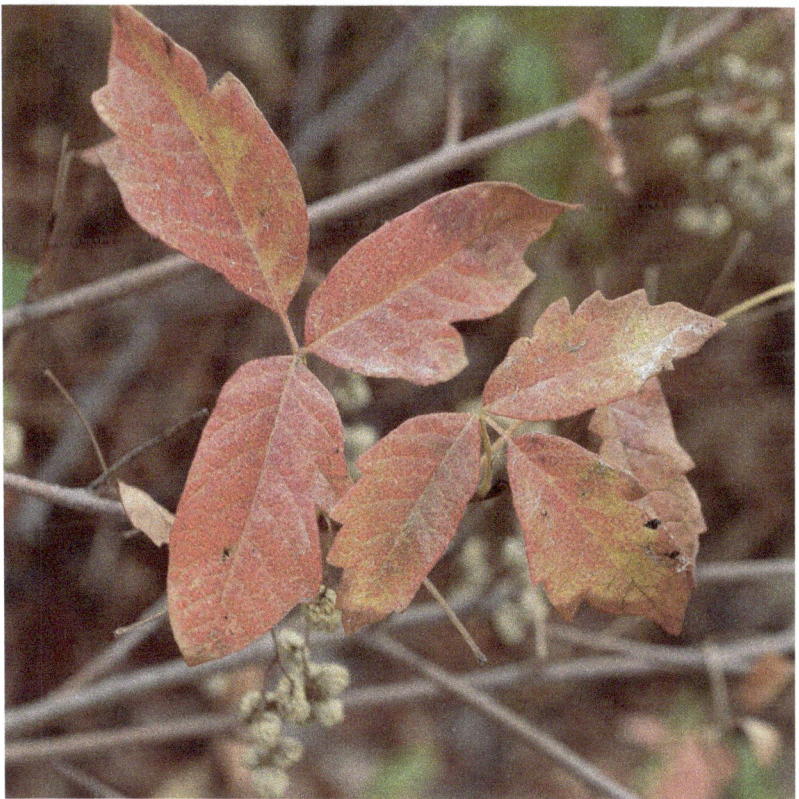

# *Trichostema lanatum* Benth.
## WOOLLY BLUE CURLS

**MINT FAMILY** (Lamiaceae)

**DESCRIPTION** Small rounded evergreen largely woody subshrub, 0.5 to 1.5 m tall, young stems square, hairy and reddish becoming brown and less hairy, mature stems with shreddy bark. **Leaves** lance-linear, 3.5 to 7.5 cm long, 1 to 6 mm wide, rolled under at edges, green above, white and fuzzy below, bundles of small leaves in axils of larger opposite pairs. **Flowers** April to August, short clusters from leaf axils along upper stems, blooms are irregular, blue and fuzzy with long stamens extending beyond corolla, blooms more or less covered with bluish pink to nearly white hairs. **Fruit**, 4 nutlets, joined at base, roughened with prominent veins and short stiff hair.

**DISTRIBUTION** Dry slopes of coastal mountains, below 1400 m (4500 ft).

**FIRE RESPONSE** Sprouting ability unknown, numerous seedlings after fire.

**WILDLIFE VALUE** Low value; honey bees use flowers.

**CULTURAL VALUE** Leaves and flowers boiled for tea to relieve stomach ailments and for various uses (Sweet 1962).

# *Turricula parryi* (Gray) J.F. Macbr.
## POODLE-DOG BUSH

**BORAGE FAMILY** (Boraginaceae)

**SYNONYM** *Eriodictyon parryi* (Gray) Greene

**DESCRIPTION** Coarse evergreen sub-shrub 1 to 2.5 m tall, glandular-hairy purplish stems becoming brown at base, sticky, ill-smelling herbage, drooping and brown with age, appearing like shaggy poodle heads. **Leaves** alternate, pubescent or hirsute, crowded, 5 to 20 cm long, 1 to 2.5 cm wide, toothed or entire, without petioles. **Flowers** June to August, numerous in a scorpiod raceme, coiled fiddleneck cluster commonly more than 10 cm long, individual flowers purple, tubular and pubescent, 13 to 18 mm long. **Fruit**, membranous capsule. Plants may be mostly herbaceous.

**DISTRIBUTION** Occasional in dry disturbed places, 300 to 2400 m (1000–8000 ft); chaparral to yellow pine communities.

**FIRE RESPONSE** Non-sprouter, profuse seedlings on burns.

**WILDLIFE VALUE** Low value, insects use flowers.

**CULTURAL VALUE** None known; contact with this plant causes some people to have dermatitis.

## Turricula parryi (Gray) J.F. Macbr.
### POODLE-DOG BUSH

# *Umbellularia californica* (Hook. & Arn.) Nutt.
## CALIFORNIA BAY (LAUREL)

**LAUREL FAMILY** (Lauraceae)

**DESCRIPTION** Normally an evergreen tree to 30 m tall or large erect shrub on exposed slopes and in chaparral, young stems with green bark turning brown with age. **Leaves** entire, simple, alternate, shiny, lance-shaped or oblong, 3 to 10 cm long, 1.5 to 4 cm wide, pungent odor when crushed. **Flowers** January through June, small, greenish yellow, 4- to 10-flowered clusters. **Fruit** greenish to dark purple round-ovoid drupe, 2 to 2.5 cm long containing hard stone.

**DISTRIBUTION** Common in canyons, shaded slopes; many plant communities from mesic chaparral to dense woodlands; mostly below 1500 m (5000 ft).

**FIRE RESPONSE** Vigorous stump and crown sprouts after fire, cutting.

**WILDLIFE VALUE** Low value browse. Fruits eaten by Steller's jays and similar birds.

**CULTURAL VALUE** Leaves can be dried and used as condiment. Inhaling too much of aromatic leaves can cause headaches. Native Americans used leaves to cure headaches by placing piece of leaf in nostril and binding several leaves to forehead (Clarke 1977).

# *Umbellularia californica* (Hook. & Arn.) Nutt.
## CALIFORNIA BAY (LAUREL)

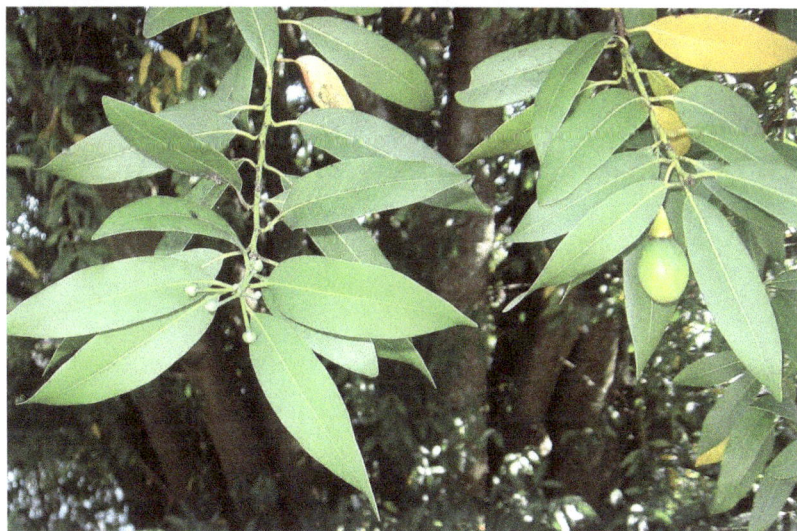

# *Venegasia carpesioides* DC.
## CANYON SUNFLOWER

**SUNFLOWER FAMILY** (Asteraceae)

**DESCRIPTION** Erect perennial herbs from a woody base, to 2.5 m tall, young stems purplish to brown becoming more definitely brown with age, stem has pith center, stems and leaves sparingly pubescent. **Leaves**, thin, alternate and simple, 3 to 15 cm long, 1.5 to 12 cm wide, large serrations, notched at base and somewhat heart-shaped, sometimes lobed, usually darker green above. **Flowers** March through August, blooms are large heads with 13 to 20 yellow female ray-flowers 15 to 20 mm long, many male tube flowers. **Fruit**, achene.

**DISTRIBUTION** Shaded canyon walls, coastal to 800 m (2700 ft); coastal sage scrub (soft chaparral), scrub oak chaparral.

**FIRE RESPONSE** Seedlings.

**WILDLIFE VALUE** Birds eat the seeds.

**CULTURAL VALUE** None known.

# *Vitis girdiana* Munson
## DESERT WILD GRAPE

**GRAPE FAMILY** (Vitaceae)

**DESCRIPTION** Deciduous shrub with trailing tendril bearing stems climbing over and supported by other plants or may be bush-like, young stems with some hairyness becoming brown with age. **Leaves**, simple, alternate, green to light green, darker above, 3 or 5 veins from heart-shaped base, ovate in outline but tips tend to be triangular, lobed and coarsely serrate, with cobwebby hairs beneath, 5 to 10 cm long, 5 to 16 cm wide, petioles 3 to 5 cm long. **Flowers** May and June, small, fragrant, greenish blossoms in racemes to 12 cm long. **Fruit**, smooth, blackish berry, 3 to 6 mm diameter.

**DISTRIBUTION** Along streams, canyon bottoms below 1200 m (4000 ft); scrub oak chaparral, live oak woodland, coastal sage scrub (soft chaparral).

**FIRE RESPONSE** Information not available, probably root sprouts if not too severely burned.

**WILDLIFE VALUE** Berries staple for birds and animals.

**CULTURAL VALUE** Native Americans ate berries raw or dried and stored them. Juice of grape leaves used to treat diarrhea and "lust in women" (Clarke 1977).

# *Vitis girdiana* Munson
## DESERT WILD GRAPE

# *Xylococcus bicolor* Nutt.
## MISSION MANZANITA

**HEATH FAMILY** (Ericaceae)

**DESCRIPTION** Erect evergreen shrub to 3 m tall, shredded reddish to gray-brown bark. **Leaves** lanceolate to ovate or obovate, alternate, dark green and shiny above, often with obvious vein indentations, whitish and pubescent to tomentose below, thick and leathery, involute or at least rolled under at margins, tapering at both ends, 3 to 6 cm long, 1 to 2 cm wide, petiole 0.5 to 1 cm long. **Flowers** December to March, white or pink urn-shaped blossoms, 8 to 9 mm long. **Fruit**, black or reddish dry drupe, 5 to 8 mm diameter, containing hard stone.

**DISTRIBUTION** Below 600 m (2000 ft); chamise chaparral and ceanothus chaparral.

**FIRE RESPONSE** Stump or crown sprouts after fire, cutting.

**WILDLIFE VALUE** Low value browse and fruit.

**CULTURAL VALUE** None known.

# *Yucca* spp.
## YUCCAS

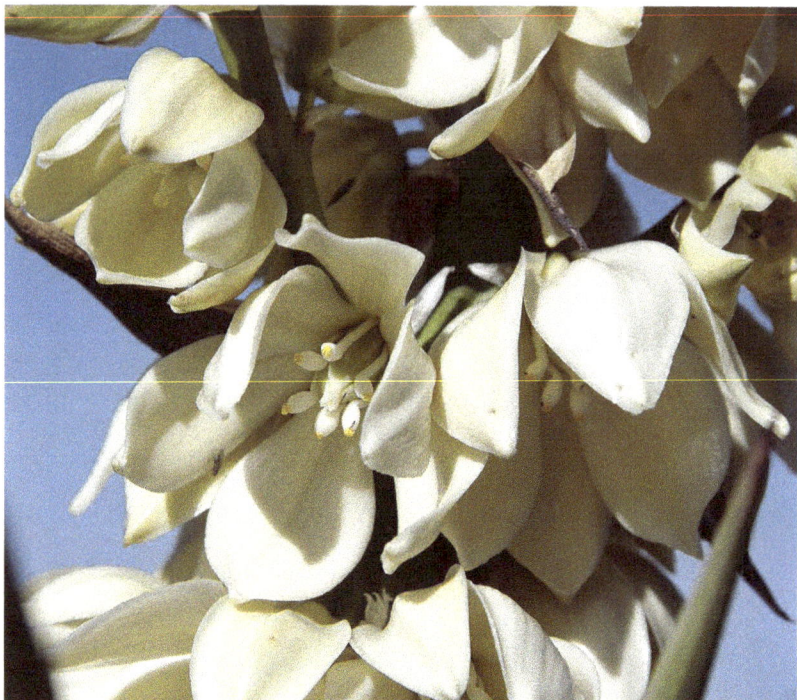

**SPANISH BAYONET**
(*Yucca schidigera*), flowers.

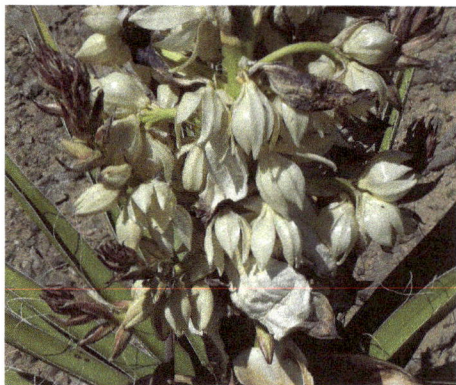

**ASPARAGUS FAMILY** (Asparagaceae)

### Key to Yucca

**1a**. Leaves gray green, with sharp, black spine at the tips, never with stringy edges; common in dry coastal sage scrub, chaparral, creosote bush between 300 and 2400 m. . . . . . . . . . . . . . . . . . . . . . . . . . . . . **CHAPARRAL YUCCA**, *Y. whipplei*

**1b**. Leaves with stringy edges; occasional on dry inland slopes on both sides of the mountains below 1500 m. . . . . . . . . . . . . . **SPANISH BAYONET**, *Y. schidigera*

**CHAPARRAL YUCCA** (*Yucca whipplei*).

# *Yucca schidigera* Roezl ex Ortgies
## SPANISH DAGGER

**ASPARAGUS FAMILY** (Asparagaceae, formerly placed in Agave Family, Agavaceae)

**DESCRIPTION** Stiff-leaved, robust plant with short trunk. **Leaves** concave or flattened, green to greenish yellow with brown tip, to 1 m long, 2 to 6 cm wide, sharp-pointed spine tip, stringy edges. **Flowers** March to June, on extended stalk to 30 cm long (short compared with *Y. whipplei*), blossoms whitish with purple tinge, bell-shaped, to 4 cm long. **Fruit**, capsule to 11 cm long, 4 cm wide. Pollination done only by yucca moth (*Pronuba* sp.).

**DISTRIBUTION** Dry rocky slopes, below 1500 m (5000 ft); both sides of southern California mountains, Mojave Desert, San Bernardino Valley, San Jacinto, Santa Rosa Mountains south to San Diego, and Baja California. On desert side, **Joshua tree**, *Y. brevifolia* Engelm., root-sprouts after fire and may appear shrubby at that time.

**FIRE RESPONSE** Root-sprouts after fire, cutting.

**WILDLIFE VALUE** Low value browse. Indicator of severe range problems if eaten by cattle.

**CULTURAL VALUE** Fruits of chaparral yucca edible. Leaves used for cordage, leaf tips could be used as a needle.

## *Yucca schidigera* Roezl ex Ortgies
## SPANISH DAGGER

# *Yucca whipplei* Torr.
## CHAPARRAL YUCCA

**ASPARAGUS FAMILY** (Asparagaceae, formerly placed in Agave Family, Agavaceae)

**SYNONYM** Now often classified as *Hesperoyucca whipplei* (Torr.) Baker

**DESCRIPTION** A stiff-leaved robust plant, apparently stemless, has tall flower stalk with massive fruiting panicle. **Leaves** all basal, bright green to gray green with brown spine tip, 0.3 to 1 m long, 0.8 to 1.0 cm wide, more or less flattened or concave, rigid, slender terminal spine 1 to 2 cm long; flower stalk sprouting from base, to 2.5 m tall. **Flowers** April and May, cream white, or tinged purple, open bell-shaped, 2 to 4 cm long. **Fruit**, capsule about 4 cm long and 3 cm across. After fruiting is complete, entire aerial part of plant dies and regeneration may occur from seed or short rhizomes or stolons. Pollination only by small yucca moth (*Pronuba* sp.).

**DISTRIBUTION** Dry slopes, 300 to 2400 m (1000–8000 ft); coastal sage scrub (soft chaparral), creosote bush, manzanita, to chamise chaparral; Monterey County, southern Sierra Nevadas to southern California.

**FIRE RESPONSE** Basal resprouts if not too severely burned and a burned stand frequently produces a profusion of flowers in a year or two after fire.

**WILDLIFE VALUE** Low value browse, fruits eaten by birds and insects.

**CULTURAL VALUE** Fruits and flowers edible (Clarke 1977).

# *Yucca whipplei* Torr.
CHAPARRAL YUCCA

Abrams, LeRoy. *Illustrated flora of the Pacific States.* 4 v. Palo Alto, CA: Stanford Univ. Press; 1960. 2791 p.

Baldwin, Bruce G. (Editor) et al. *The Jepson Manual Vascular Plants of California* (2nd ed.). Berkeley: Univ. of California Press; 2012. 1600 p. Also see: *The Jepson eFlora* (https://ucjeps.berkeley.edu/eflora).

Balls, Edward K. *Early uses of California plants.* Berkeley: Univ. of California Press; 1972. 103 p.

Clarke, Charlotte Bringle. *Edible and useful plants of California.* Berkeley: Univ. of California Press; 1977. 280 p.

Collins, Barbara J. *Key to coastal and chaparral flowering plants of southern California.* Northridge, CA: California Lutheran College; 1974a. 249 p.

Collins, Barbara J. *Key to trees and wildflowers of the mountains of southern California.* Northridge, CA: California Lutheran College; 1974b. 277 p.

Hanes, Ted L. *Ecological studies on two closely related chaparral shrubs in southern California.* Ecological Monographs 35(2):213-235; 1965 Spring.

Martin, A. C.; Zim, H. S.; Nelson, A. L. *American wildlife and plants; a guide to wildlife food habits.* New York: Dover Publ., Inc.; 1951. 500 p.

Mason, Herbert L. *A Flora of the Marshes of California.* Berkeley: Univ. of California Press; 1957. 878 p.

McMinn, Howard E. *An illustrated manual of California shrubs.* Berkeley: Univ. of California Press; 1939. 663 p.

Medsger. Oliver Perry. *Edible wild plants.* New York: Collier MacMillan Publishers; 1966. 323 p.

Munz, Philip A. *A flora of southern California.* Berkeley: Univ. of California Press; 1974. 1086 p.

Munz, Philip A.; Keck, David. *A California flora and supplement.* Berkeley: Univ. of California Press; 1970. 1681 p.

Raven, Peter H. *Native shrubs of southern California.* Berkeley: Univ. of California Press; 1966. 132 p.

Smith, Clifton F. *A flora of the Santa Barbara region.* Santa Barbara: Santa Barbara Museum of Natural History; 1976. 331 p.

Stebbins, G. L.; Major, J. *Endemism and speciation flora.* Ecological Monographs 35(1):1-35; 1965 Winter.

Sweet, Muriel. *Common edible and useful plants of the west.* Healdsburg, CA: Naturegraph Co.; 1962. 64 p.

U.S. Department of Agriculture, Forest Service. *Range analysis.* FSH 2209.21. San Francisco: Div. Range and Wildlife Manage., California Region, Forest Service, U.S. Department of Agriculture; 1969 [Loose leaf, updated].

Van Dersal, William R. *Native woody plants of the United States.* Misc. Publ. No. 303. Washington, DC; U.S. Department of Agriculture; 1938. 362 p.

# LEAF CHARACTERS

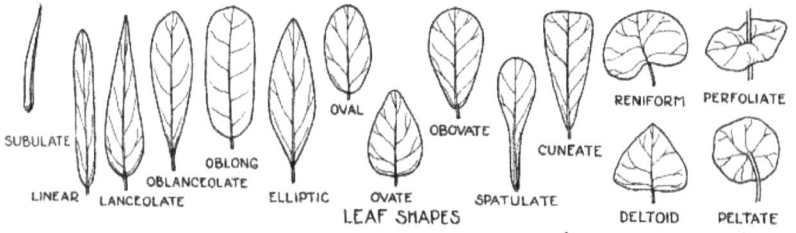

SUBULATE · LINEAR · LANCEOLATE · OBLONG · OBLANCEOLATE · ELLIPTIC · OVAL · OVATE · OBOVATE · SPATULATE · CUNEATE · RENIFORM · PERFOLIATE · DELTOID · PELTATE

LEAF SHAPES

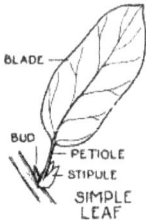

BLADE
BUD
PETIOLE
STIPULE
SIMPLE LEAF

PALMATELY COMPOUND

PINNATELY COMPOUND

BIPINNATELY COMPOUND

DISSECTED

DECOMPOUND

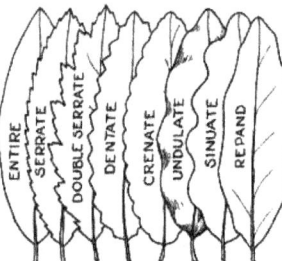

ENTIRE · SERRATE · DOUBLE SERRATE · DENTATE · CRENATE · UNDULATE · SINUATE · REPAND

MARGINS

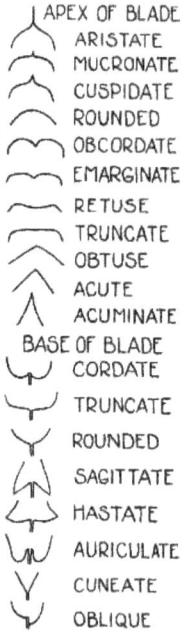

APEX OF BLADE
ARISTATE
MUCRONATE
CUSPIDATE
ROUNDED
OBCORDATE
EMARGINATE
RETUSE
TRUNCATE
OBTUSE
ACUTE
ACUMINATE
BASE OF BLADE
CORDATE
TRUNCATE
ROUNDED
SAGITTATE
HASTATE
AURICULATE
CUNEATE
OBLIQUE

PINNATELY LOBED

PINNATELY CLEFT

PINNATELY PARTED

PINNATELY DIVIDED

PALMATELY LOBED

PALMATELY CLEFT

PALMATELY PARTED

PALMATELY DIVIDED

Leaf characters (Mason, 1957).

**Abrupt**: Terminates suddenly without taper.

**Acuminate**: leaf tapers to a point which may be sharp.

**Acute**: Less taper than acuminate but with a sharp point.

**Achene**: A small fruit which does not break open when it matures but does become dry and hard.

**Alternate**: Generally indicates one leaf per node, can also be applied to other parts.

**Appressed**: Pressed against another part or organ.

**Aromatic**: Fragrant with spicy, pungent, pleasant, or ill-smelling odor.

**Auricle**: An appendage like an ear (lobe) especially at the base of an organ.

**Auriculate**: Having an auricle.

**Awl-shaped**: Narrow, may be nearly round and tapering to a point.

**Bark**: External covering or rind of a woody stem or root usually fibrous or cork-like and often with outer scales.

**Basal**: Relative to or at the base.

**Bipinnate**: Doubly or twice pinnate.

**Bluff**: Geographic feature rising steeply to a flat or rounded front; for example, at a coast line.

**Bract**: Appendage(s) below flowers formed by a reduced leaf usually at the base of a flower pedicel.

**Bractlet**: A bract borne on a pedicel rather than at the base; for example, below the sepals of roses.

**Branch**: A shoot or secondary stem growing from a larger stem.

**Branchlet**: Generally the ultimate or final and smallest branch.

**Broom-like**: Resembling the household implement for sweeping; branches end with several slender branchlets with small leaves.

**Burl**: A lump at the base of the stem and at the root crown which has many buds from which sprouts may arise.

**Bush**: A shrub, especially one with thick, dense branching.

**Canescent**: Covered with whitish or grayish fine hairs.

**Capsule**: Fruit with two or more seeds, splits open when mature and dry.

**Catkin**: An open or tight cluster of small scale-like or bearded unisexual flowers in a string resembling a cat's tail; also called an "ament."

**Chaparral**: Shrub formation generally composed of dense shrubs (sometimes nearly impenetrable) with small, hard leaves (sclerophylls).

**Coastal**: Geographic location near the seashore with climate influenced by proximity to the ocean.

**Compound**: An organ having two or more similar parts.

**Conifers**: Cone-bearing plants; trees or shrubs with needle or scale-like leaves.

**Convolute**: Rolled upwards longitudinally.

**Cordate**: Heart-shaped, with the notch at the base and ovate in general outline.

**Coriaceous**: Cough like leather, especially in texture and feel.

**Crenate**: Leaf margin has rounded projections and scalloped look.

**Crisped**: Irregularly curled or wavy, ripples.

**Cuneate**: Wedge shaped, tapered toward the base.

**Cupped**: In the form of a cup or with edges more or less turned up to form a bowl.

**Cyme**: A flowering cluster which is more or less flat-topped; blooms mature from the center out, and the central axis ends with a flower.

# GLOSSARY OF TERMS

**Cymose:** Bearing one or more cyme.

**Deciduous:** Denotes to leaves that fall or are shed at a particular season

**Decumbent:** Lying down on the ground with the tips turning up.

**Deltoid:** Delta shaped, an equal sided triangle.

**Dentate:** Margin is cut with sharp teeth not pointed forward.

**Denticulate:** Margin is finely toothed.

**Dermatitis:** A skin rash.

**Desert:** Region of low rainfall with sparse vegetation except where supplemental moisture is provided as along streams and seeps.

**Dioecious:** Plant species that have male and female flowers on different plants.

**Divergent:** Extending away at a steep angle: divaricate divergence is especially wide.

**Divided:** Separated to base.

**Drought-deciduous:** Referring to woody plants that shed leaves in response to inadequate moisture supply.

**Drupe:** Fleshy fruit enclosing a single hard stone containing a seed, e.g. a stone fruit such as a peach.

**Elliptic:** Leaf shaped like an ellipse - more than twice as long as broad and widest at the center.

**Emarginate:** A leaf or petal with a small notch at the tip.

**Entire:** An unbroken margin, not toothed or serrated.

**Epidermis:** The outer layer of cells form the skin of plant parts.

**Erect:** Generally upright with respect to the ground but also implies an organ which is perpendicular to a stem or leaf surface.

**Evergreen:** Retains green leaves year-round.

**Fascicle:** Close cluster or bundle of flowers leaves, stems, or roots.

**Feather-veined:** Veins arise from the sides of the midrib.

**Forest:** Dense growth of trees and shrubs covering the landscape; tree cover greater than woodland.

**Genus:** Taxonomic classification category between family and species; the first word in the Latin name of a species and is capitalized.

**Glabrous:** Refers only to the lack of hairy ness, bald.

**Gland:** An organ represented by a depression or protuberance for secreting fluids (sometimes in very small amounts).

**Glandular:** Bearing gland or gland-like structures.

**Glaucous:** More or less covered with a white or gray powder that can be rubbed off.

**Globose:** Spherical or roundish.

**Glutinous:** Waxy or gluey appearing surface formed by an exudate.

**Half-shrub:** Used as a synonym for subshrub; between a shrub and a herbaceous plant, having herbaceous stems that are shed with leaves or flowers.

**Herbaceous:** Plants or plant parts having the texture and color of leaves; plants that die to the ground after completing annual growth cycles.

**Hirsute:** Covered more or less densely with coarse distinctive hairs.

**Hispid:** Rough with stiff or bristly hairs.

**Hoary:** Covered with white down.

**Inflorescence:** Characteristic arrangement and disposition of flowers on a plant.

**Interior**: Inland, here meaning removed from the coast far enough to reduce influence from the ocean.

**Internode**: That portion of stem between two nodes.

**Lanceolate**: Lance-shaped leaf, much longer than broad (usually more than 3 times) tapering from below the middle to the tip.

**Lateral**: On the side or coming from the sides.

**Leaf**: Outgrowth from a plant stem, in several forms, but most frequently flat.

**Leaflet**: Subunit or segment of a compound leaf.

**Leathery**: Resembles leather in appearance and feel, may be associated with the stiff and or thick characteristics of sclerophylls (harsh-leaved).

**Linear**: Leaf sides parallel like a blade of grass; linear leaves tend to be long and narrow.

**Lobe**: Division or segment of an organ, usually rounded or obtuse; cut less than halfway to the leaf midrib.

**Margin**: Border or edge of a structure.

**Midrib**: Central rib or vein of a leaf.

**Midvein**: Variant of midrib; the central rib of an organ such as a leaf.

**Monoecious**: Plant species that have male and female flowers on the same plant.

**Montane**: Pertaining to mountains.

**Mucronate**: With a short sharp pointed tip at the end of 'a leaf.

**Node**: Joint of a stem; the point where lateral buds and leaves arise on a stem.

**Oblanceolate**: Broadest part of the leaf between mid-leaf and the outer end; tapers gradually toward the petiole. usually rounded abruptly at the end, similar to spatulate.

**Oblique**: Sides of unequal length.

**Oblong**: Leaf much longer than broad, sides nearly parallel.

**Obovate**: Reverse of ovate, with the wide end toward the leaf tip.

**Obtuse**: Blunt or rounded at the end.

**Opposite**: Set against, as with two leaves at a node.

**Orbicular**: Circular and flat.

**Oval**: Broad, elliptic leaf with rounded ends.

**Ovate**: Leaf shaped like the outline of a hen's egg with the big end near the base.

**Palmate**: Hand-shaped with the fingers spread; in a leaf, lobes or veins radiate from a common point.

**Peduncle**: Stalk of an inflorescence; the stalk between a flower and the plant stem.

**Perfect flower**: Flowers with both male and female parts (stamens and pistils).

**Pericarp**: Ripe walls of the ovary; often in several layers, as in a peach which includes a hard endocarp next to the seed, the mesocarp or flesh of the fruit, and the epicarp or skin of the fruit.

**Petiole**: Leafstalk which supports the leaf blade and connects to the plant stem.

**Pinnate**: Having the leaflets or veins arranged on each side of a common petiole, midrib or central vein; feather-like.

**Prickle**: Sharp outgrowth of the bark or epidermis.

**Prickly**: Covered with prickles.

**Prostrate**: Lying flat upon the ground.

**Prussic acid**: Hydrocyanic acid is a weak acid, hence an acrid but not unpleasant peach blossom odor.

**Puberulent**: Minutely hairy, finely pubescent.

# GLOSSARY OF TERMS

**Pubescent**: Any plant part more or less covered with short, soft hair.

**Raceme**: Inflorescence with flowers on stalks (pedicels) along a main axis in a dense or open, upright or drooping arrangement.

**Resin**: Amorphous yellow to brown to transparent covering or exudate.

**Resinous**: Having the characteristics of resin, as in leaves with resinous surfaces.

**Revolute**: Leaf rolled downward from both margins; that is, toward the underside.

**Rhizome**: Rootlike stem usually growing underground, mostly parallel with the soil surface and giving rise to roots from the lower side and shoots from the upper side.

**Rib**: (midrib) Primary vein of a leaf, or a ridge on a fruit.

**Riperian**: Along a stream, lake, or spring.

**Rush-like**: Resembling a rush; more or less straight greenish stems with few or no leaves.

**Sage**: Group of aromatic shrub or subshrub species belonging to the *Salvia* genus in the mint family.

**Sage-scrub**: A subshrub formation generally found near the coast to about 1000 m (3300 ft).

**Scarious**: Thin and membranous in texture as a scarious bract.

**Scale-like**: Any thin scarious bract, usually a vestigial leaf.

**Sclerophyllous**: Refers to the leaves; meaning hard, indurate. The common shrubs of chaparral have hard leathery leaves.

**Scurfy**: Covered with small flaky scales, branlike.

**Sepal**: A leaf or segment of a flower's calyx.

**Serrate**: Sawtoothed leaf margin; teeth pointing forward.

**Sessile**: Stalkless. attached directly at the base; sessile leaves lack a petiole.

**Shreddy**: Coming off in narrow strips; shreddy bark.

**Shrub**: A woody plant, smaller than a tree and generally with multiple branching near the ground.

**Simple**: Not branched or compound.

**Sinuate**: Leaf with a wavy indented margin similar to crenate.

**Smooth**: Not rough to touch; without hairs or other rough material.

**Spatulate**: Spatula shaped, similar to oblanceolate; along blade rounded at both ends, but tapers toward the base from above the middle.

**Species**: Latin or "scientific" taxonomic name for a group of plants that have characteristics more specific than genus but less than sub species or variety; abbreviated sp. for singular and spp. for plural.

**Spine**: Sharp-pointed, stiff, woody body, arising from below the epidermis, usually a modified leaf.

**Sprawling**: Spreading irregularly along the ground or in and over other plants.

**Stem**: Any stalk or structure which supports a more distant part of a plant as a leaf, flower, or plant canopy.

**Stipule**: Appendage (usually two) at the base of a leaf petiole, a modified or undeveloped leaf often reminiscent of an ear.

**Stolon**: A stem usually growing along the ground surface (sometimes just below the surface) that gives rise to roots and shoots.

**Strigose**: Clothed with sharp appressed hairs.

**Subshrub**: Synonym for half-shrub; that is, between a shrub and a herbaceous plant, having herbaceous stems that are shed with leaves or flowers.

**Subspecies**: Taxonomic division of species; that is, more specific than species and with consistent minor differences between subspecies; abbreviated ssp.

**Sufrutescent**: Somewhat or obscurely woody, but not necessarily low stature.

**Suffruticose**: Somewhat woody with low stature.

**Ternate**: Arranged in groups of three, as a leaf consisting of three leaflets.

**Taxon**: A taxonomic unit such as variety, species, family, etc.

**Taxa**: Plural of taxon.

**Thorn**: Stiff and sharp-pointed like a spine but a thorn is a modified branch.

**Tomentose**: Covered with a mat (tomentum) of short dense hairs appearing wool-like.

**Tomentulose**: Minutely tomentose.

**Tooth**: Small, usually pointed lobe on a leaf margin.

**Tree**: Perennial woody plant generally limited to one or a few stems at the base, with a mature height greater than 3 m (10 ft) tall.

**Truncate**: Ending abruptly as if cut off, not tapering.

**Twig**: A small diameter branch; diameter of less than 0.6 cm (0.25 in) is implied in this guide.

**Undulate**: Wavy.

**Utricle**: Indehiscent (does not split at maturity) fruit composed of a pouch-like, membranous pericarp enclosing the seed.

**Variety**: A taxonomic division of species; approximately the same meaning as subspecies; abbreviated var.

**Vein**: Vascular conductive bundle of a leaf or other flat organ.

**Venation**: Arrangement of the veins of a leaf.

**Vestigial**: Adjective implying evovled to a trace of a part once more perfectly developed.

**Villous**: Covered with shaggy hair not especially matted.

**Vine**: A plant whose stems depend on objects or other plants for support.

**Viscid**: Sticky or glutinous.

**Whorl**: Ring of similar organs radiating from a node as several leaves arising from a stem node.

**Woodland**: Land covered with trees and shrubs. Woodland implies land with tree cover less than a forest.

**Woody**: Stems and twigs are ligneous (wood) rather than herbaceous and do not die back to the ground after completing annual growth.

**Woolly**: Having long, soft hairs; usually more or less matted.

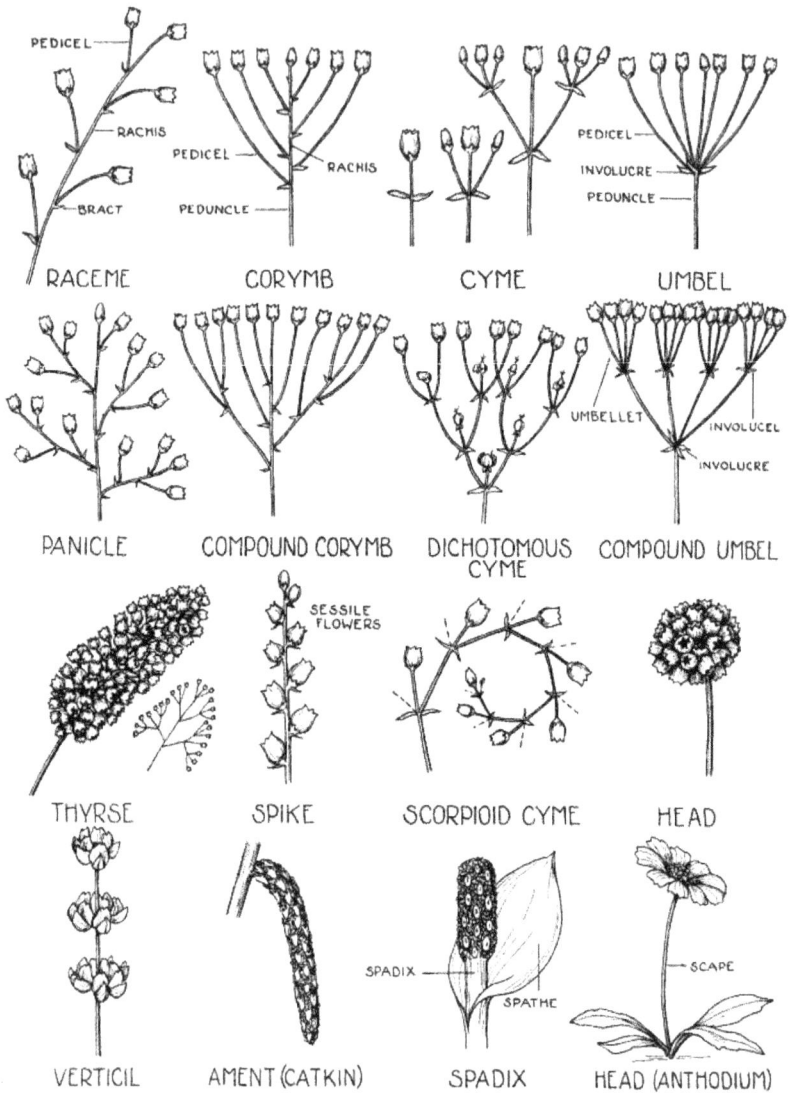

Inflorescence types. (Mason, 1957).

# ACKNOWLEDGMENTS

This book is largely based on *Common Shrubs of Chaparral and Associated Ecosystems of Southern California,* published by the Pacific Southwest Forest and Range Experiment Station, Berkeley, California, as General Technical Report PSW-99 (1987). The present guide has been revised and updated to reflect current taxonomic nomenclature, and color illustrations and distribution maps have been added.

Photographs were obtained, where possible, from public domain sources, from the author's own collection, and from a number of photographers on Flickr who have made their work available under Creative Commons commercial use licences (see www.flickr.com). Detailed plant illustrations were generated from herbarium specimens housed at a number of herbaria in the United States. Grateful acknowledgment is given to the Biota of North America Project (*www.bonap.org*) for permission to use their data to generate the distribution maps.

The principal author of the 1987 work was C. Eugene Conrad (1930-2014). Conrad was formerly in charge of the research unit in the Station's research and development program titled "Vegetation Management Alternatives for Chaparral and related Ecosystems," headquartered at the Forest Fire Laboratory, Riverside, Calif. He later headed the Forest Management Research Unit at Honolulu, Hawaii. He earned bachelor's (1956) and master's (1959) degrees from Oregon State University. He joined the Forest Service and Station's research staff in 1961.

# PUBESCENCE TYPES

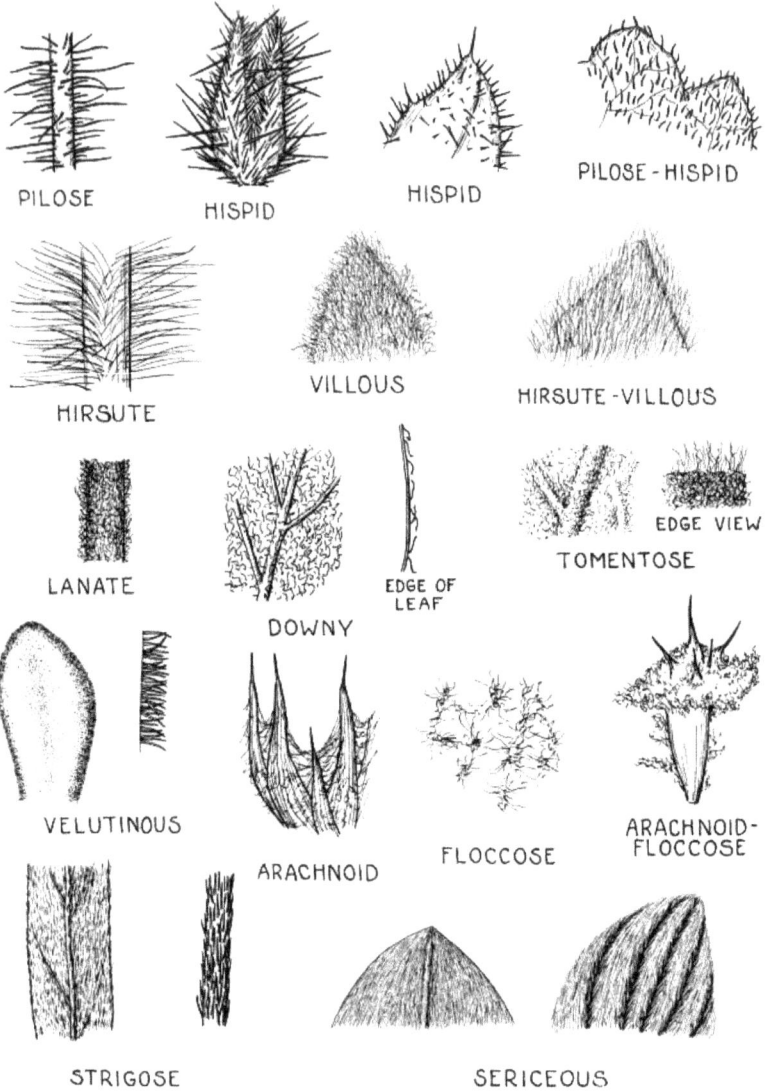

Pubescence types. (Mason, 1957).

# INDEX BY PLANT FAMILY

**BUSHRUE** (*Cneoridium dumosum*), page 110.

# INDEX BY COMMON NAME

# INDEX BY SCIENTIFIC NAME

# INDEX BY SCIENTIFIC NAME

337